W9-BGL-002

THE WORLDS MOST POWERFUL CARS

THE WORLDS MOST
POWERFUL
CARS

GRAHAM ROBSON

CHARTWELL
BOOKS, INC.

A QUINTET BOOK

Published by Chartwell Books
A Division of Book Sales, Inc.
110 Enterprise Avenue
Secaucus, New Jersey 07094

ISBN 1-55521-563-7

This book was designed and produced by
Quintet Publishing Limited
6 Blundell Street
London N7 9BH

Creative Director: Peter Bridgewater
Art Director: Ian Hunt
Designer: James Lawrence
Artwork: Danny McBride
Editor: Shaun Barrington

Typeset in Great Britain by
Central Southern Typesetters, Eastbourne
Manufactured in Hong Kong by
Regent Publishing Services Limited
Printed in Hong Kong by
Leefung-Asco Printers Limited

Contents

Introduction

Right from the start of the motoring era, more than a hundred years ago, powerful men have loved powerful cars. Although there was never any logical reason for believing it, anyone whose car was faster and more powerful than the others felt that he was more important, and more powerful too. Maybe Mandell Creighton, who wrote in 1904: **'Power tends to corrupt, and absolute power corrupts absolutely . . .'** knew a thing or two!

There can be a vast difference, of course, between powerful cars and fast cars, but usually the two features go together.

Traditionally, engine power has been measured as brake horse power (bhp), though in recent years (because of metrication) it has also been quoted in kilowatts. While few of the old school can understand kilowatts, even a thoroughly modern 'metric' enthusiast can understand brake horsepower, and that's the way I quote power ratings in this book. Only a few countries (including Australia), have officially discarded 'bhp'. Lovers of tradition can relax!

The power of a horse (lifting weights out of a mine shaft) was measured in the 18th century, when someone needed to compare this with the effort they were getting from new-fangled steam engines. Brake horsepower has always been measured, to the same standards, on test machines called 'brakes'.

Sixty years ago we looked on an engine which produced more than 150bhp as amazing, 30 years ago we thought 300bhp engines were special, and nowadays we look on 500bhp and more as simply awesome. In the same period, engines have become more and more fuel efficient – and smaller. Today's family runabout engine is as powerful as those fitted to gargantuan Mercedes sports cars early in the century. A modern 3.5–litre Ferrari is as powerful as the 12.7–litre Bugatti Royale of the 1920s.

But is there any end in sight? Race cars, after all, have already used more than 1000bhp in Formula One, and sports car events; in recent years they have been using less and less fuel than before. Drag racing machines, using weird fuel mixes, produce untold power. The limits of turbocharging have not yet been reached. So where do we go from here?

Powerful engines – the questions and the answers . . .

Every motoring enthusiast knows all about engine design. Or does he? Is it air or fuel that burns to produce power? Is it engine size or engine speed which creates power? Here, then, is a very brief lesson in engine design.

A car engine produces power by making controlled explosions, which turn the rotating parts, and thus drive the road wheels. Torque is produced by using force to turn a drive shaft, but power is produced by turning that shaft at high speeds.

The car that changed the face of motoring was the 35hp Mercedes of 1901 – three years later the same basic engine was on sale with double that power – 70bhp. The power race was well and truly underway.

The explosions are caused by burning various types of fuel in cylinders; in almost every case, the fuel is petrol, distilled from oil. Burning requires oxygen, which is freely available from the air. To increase power, more fuel has to be burnt efficiently. In the early years, the way to do this was simply to use more air in larger cylinders – which meant making the engines bigger and heavier.

That was easy enough, but the practical limit was soon reached. The difficult task, with which engine designers all over the world are still grappling, is that cars had to be made lighter, smaller, faster and cheaper. This meant that they needed more power from smaller, lighter, and more efficient engines, this often being achieved by having more, smaller cylinders.

Power, efficiency and performance

Look at it this way. A lot of power is not always enough. A big truck, after all, sometimes has as much power as a Ferrari, but there are vast differences in 'performance.'

There are two major factors to consider – one is a rating called the power/weight ratio, and the other is the car's aerodynamic efficiency. Put simply, this means that a lightweight car with 300bhp will always perform better than a heavyweight with the same engine. Furthermore, a car with a smooth and slippery aerodynamic style (and a small frontal area) will always go faster than a behemoth with a craggy style – the Jaguar XKE would always outpace a Cadillac, even with less power.

At the same time, an engine's efficiency is measured by the amount of power it develops relative to its cubic capacity. Cubic capacity is defined in two ways – most of the world's nations measure an engine in litres, but in North America (the largest car marketplace in the world) engines are measured in cubic inches. In this book, I have quoted both measures for each engine.

Engine efficiency, therefore, is measured either in bhp/litre (European), or as bhp/cubic inch (North America). Both ratings, of course, have shown steady improvements over the hundred years in which cars have been on sale.

Although it was still high, and simply engineered, the Mercedes sports cars of the early 1900s were a dramatic advance on the pioneering machines of the 1890s.

FAR LEFT ABOVE
Early cars, like this Ford Model A of 1903, had top speeds of around 30-40mph. In those days no-one could believe that 200mph top speeds would be available before the end of the 1980s.

LEFT
Fiat's original 3½hp car of 1899 was only able to jog along at the speed of a horse. A 1980s Ferrari F40 would have more than 130 times as much power!

engineers have been forced to look deeper and deeper into the chemistry, the aerodynamics and the electronics of motor car engine control.

Producing the power – a century of technical advance

The vast majority of the world's cars have been powered by piston engines, and the principle of such units was established by two European inventors – Etienne Lenoir and

In particular, engineers have learned a lot about improving the flow of air, fuel, and burnt exhaust gases, into and out of the cylinders. Not only have they increased flow-efficiency, but they have encouraged engines to revolve faster and faster as well. The layout and number of the valves and the shape of all the gas passages have continued to improve.

Furthermore, for a given engine capacity, the engineers discovered that more cylinders meant better combustion, and a faster-revving engine. On the other hand, it inevitably led to increased costs. Throughout the ages, therefore, there has been a constant battle between the engineers, the sales force and the accountants.

Technical advance has led to better, more complete, and more rapid combustion, while fuel economy ratings have improved alongside this. The days of the powerful but thirsty engines are now long gone. Due to ever-tightening regulations, not only to cut air pollution (the USA legislature was a pioneer in the 1960s), but in motorsport,

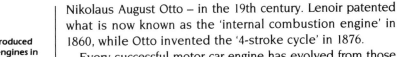

OPPOSITE
By the 1960s, not only did passenger cars have 300bhp engines, but a few (like this Jensen FF), also had four wheel drive.

BOTTOM LEFT
The world's first 'Grand Prix' was won by Ferenc Szisz, driving this 90bhp Renault. The roads all around the sircuit in France were no better than those at the start-finish line.

BOTTOM
American manufacturers produced many excellent powerful engines in the 1930s. This vee-12 powered Lincoln-Zephyr is of that period.

BELOW
In the 1930s the way to get more power was to use complex engines. This British Brough Superior model (bodied by Charlesworth) used an American Lincoln-Zephyr vee-12 engine.

Nikolaus August Otto – in the 19th century. Lenoir patented what is now known as the 'internal combustion engine' in 1860, while Otto invented the '4-stroke cycle' in 1876.

Every successful motor car engine has evolved from those principles, and the limits have certainly not been reached. The 4-stroke cycle – air/fuel mixture drawn into a cylinder, then compressed, then ignited to produce power, then exhausted – has occasionally been challenged by the less-efficient (but simpler) 2-stroke cycle, and at one time the continuous flow of the gas turbine was thought to have promise, but it still reigns supreme.

Steam engines? Far too bulky, slow-running, and inefficient. Wankel rotary engines? New in the 1960s, getting better all the time in the 1980s, but essentially these are 4-stroke engines which transmit their power to a crankshaft in different ways.

Pioneers

In the 1880s and 1890s, when the motor car was in its infancy, the miracle was not that engines worked well, but that they worked at all. Although the principles of the 4-stroke engine were well-established, there were enormous practical difficulties.

Cylinder blocks and heads were still in heavy cast iron, every component was crude and massive, the result being that it was still very difficult to make engines rotate quickly. Engineers still struggled to turn low-octane fuel into vapour, and had great problems in producing the right ignition spark (to explode fuel/air mixtures) at the right time.

Before 1900, any engine which produced 20bhp was considered powerful, which meant that a car top speed of 30–40mph (48–64kmh) was considered to be amazing. Engines had valves mounted alongside the cylinders (Europeans called this a 'side-valve' arrangement, Americans an 'L-head' or a 'T-head' depending on the detail layout), so that breathing and combustion was poor. Most engines had one or two cylinders. Four-cylinder engines were rare, and sixes were unknown.

Then, in 1901, Daimler-Benz introduced the Mercedes marque; first the 35hp, then the 60hp, and later the 90 and even the 120hp models all evolved from the same basic design of 4-cylinder overhead valve engine, and the 20th-century's power race had begun.

Cars of the future will not only be powerful, but they will also be extremely efficient. This was Mitsubishi's HSR project car of 1989.

Even so, the world's first Grand Prix winner, the Renault of 1906, had a side-valve 4-cylinder engine, needed 12.97-litres/792CID to produce 105bhp, and could revolve only at 1200rpm.

Growing up – American muscle and European sophistication

Thought it started late, North America's motor industry soon became dominant. Costs were slashed, production was boosted, and before long Detroit was producing hordes of cheap and reliable side-valve engines. Not only that, but by the 1920s companies like Cadillac (V8) and Packard (V12) were producing complex and powerful engines which caused European designers to gasp.

In Europe, on the other hand, advanced technology arrived with a flourish. To improve engine breathing, valves were put 'upstairs', and sometimes operated by an overhead camshaft mechanism. For its racing engines, Peugeot not only did this, but used two overhead camshafts. Several companies started to use four valves per cylinder, the better to get gas into and out of cylinders. With a great deal of attention to weight reduction, too, engines began to revolve much faster.

Even so, at this time the quickest and easiest way to produce a truly powerful engine was to make it larger. North America had produced some of the world's largest units in the 1910s, though the German 'Blitzen' Benz of 1909 (a racing car with a unit of 21.5 litres/1311CID, and 200bhp) made everyone sit up and think. Bugatti, however, set the limit with the magnificent 12.76-litre/779-CID 'Royale' unit, which was supposed to produce 300bhp at a mere 2000rpm.

In the 1930s, and following the great Depression which swept the world, engine sizes came down, though at the same time they became more complicated. Cadillac and Marmon produced V16 engines, while any number of makers started building straight-8s. Ultra powerful cars needed 200bhp and more to make the top table. A number of cars were sold with supercharged (forced induction) engines, though this way of tricking an engine into thinking it was larger was usually applied to smaller engines. Even so, Mercedes-Benz applied it to a whole series of massive engines, for its big limousines and its very glossy sports cars.

Post-War developments – the power race

Once the Second World War had ended, the world's car makers settled down to massive expansion of sales. Until the early 1970s oil was plentiful and cheap, and demand for new cars seemed to be insatiable, so many car makers produced larger and more powerful engines. Supercharging was abandoned, while turbocharging appeared only during the 1960s and 1970s. Fuel efficiency – which meant fuel economy – was not thought to be important.

There were two ways of producing more power:

In Europe, companies like Ferrari, Jaguar, Lamborghini and, to a lesser extent, Mercedes-Benz developed relatively small, but sophisticated, engines, all of them high-revving, some with twin overhead camshaft valve gear, and some with fuel injection. The benchmark for a truly powerful car soon soared over 200bhp again, and once cars like the 352bhp Ferrari Daytona and the 385bhp Lamborghini Miura came along, these were among the most powerful in the world.

In North America, the easiest way was to keep the engineering simple, but to build bigger engines. Why bother

RIGHT
Felix Wankel with an example of the rotary engine which bears his name, Wankel engines can rotate very fast, and produce a lot of power.

TOP RIGHT
In the 1970s and 1980s many manufacturers used forced induction – turbocharging – to improve the power output of small engines. This was the engine used in the front-drive Fiat Uno.

BOTTOM RIGHT
Ford's turbocharged 'Lima' engine was used in many corporate models.

with complex valve gear, the engineers asked, when larger engines cost little more than smaller ones? Hence the expression: 'There's no substitute for cubic inches'.

It wasn't always easy to compare Europe with America. Because the Americans tended to quote their horsepower figures in SAE measure (where none of the 'in-car' losses were deducted), their actual power was often less impressive in fact than it looked on paper. Different European countries had different standards, but most quoted what was effectively an 'installed' figure.

Even so, no one worked out how to compare, say, 300bhp of Ferrari power, with 425bhp of Corvette power. Was a 272bhp V12 Jaguar engine more, or less, powerful in fact than a 260bhp Porsche 911 Turbo unit?

The frugal 1980s – power without extravagance

After the great energy crises of 1973 and 1979, when the price of oil rocketed, and supplies sometimes threatened to dry up, most car manufacturers changed their ways.

In North America, exhaust emission regulations which required very clean exhausts strangled engines so much that Detroit's engines eventually lost 30 and sometimes 40 per cent of their 'pre-crisis' ratings. Successive generations of new models became smaller, more fuel-efficient, and a lot less powerful. By the mid-1980s, except for a few speciality sports cars like the Corvette, the USA had almost opted out of the powerful engine business.

In Europe, the same restrictions hit hard, but designers developed turbocharged engines, 4-valve cylinder heads and twin overhead camshaft valve gear. In a few outstanding cases, such as the Porsche 959 and the Ferrari F40, all

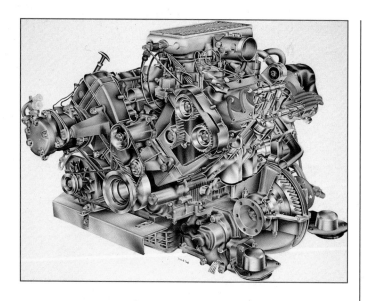

these were combined in the most remarkable way. The miracle was that such engines not only could run on less specialized fuels than before, but also could be more fuel efficient than before.

As the 1990s opened, a typical 'benchmark' figure for a supercar's engine was the 480bhp of a turbocharged 2.9-litre V8 from Ferrari – an astonishing specific output of 160bhp/litre. Is this the limit? Surely not. The 1990s are likely to be more exciting than anything before.

Maximum power – and how to get it

Over the years, an engine's efficiency has been measured in bhp/litre, and this figure has increased steadily. Early in the 20th century, any engine with 10bhp was considered advanced. By the 1920s the big Bentleys were rated at about 30bhp/litre, and ten years later, when supercharged Alfa Romeo sports cars set all the standards, 60bhp/litre was about the limit.

North American car makers rarely troubled themselves with high ratings, but opted for large and lazy engines instead. Thus, though an American car's bhp/litre figure might be relatively low, it would have a large capacity unit, and therefore a high output.

The huge advance between the wars could not, of course, be sustained. In the 1950s and 1960s, European supercars continued to set standards, for the Mercedes-Benz 300SL of 1954 had 72bhp/litre, while the Ferrari Daytona of 1968 had pushed that up to 80bhp/litre. The first normally-aspirated race car engines to touch 100bhp/litre were the Ferraris and Maseratis of the early 1950s. By the end of the 1960s, that race car figure had been raised to no less than 150bhp/litre.

In spite of the imposition of exhaust gas pollution limits and the need to use lead-free fuels and to make cars quieter, ratings have continued to increase. Turbocharging (which really means that superchargers driven by the engine's own exhaust gases are used to 'mop up' spare energy) arrived – first on Chevrolet Corvairs, then on BMW 2002s

and Porsche 911s, and later on dozens of engines. Ratings of more than 100bhp/litre became common on turbocharged roads by the late 1980s. By the end of that decade, normally-aspirated race car engines were producing 185 or even 190bhp/litre.

Many different factors help to produce such power, and all are connected with breathing efficiency and making the engine revolve faster.

Efficient combustion needs large valve areas. At least four valves per cylinder – two inlet and two exhaust – became the norm in the 1980s, while five valve heads (three inlet valves) have been tried on some smaller-engined cars. Theoretically, the more valves you can use, the more valve area you can get, but other limits are set by the complexity of valve operation and of the porting involved.

Gas flow into, inside, and out of the cylinders must be very smoothly accomplished. In spite of the existence of carefully monitored flow rigs, this is still something of a black art, and those most expert tend to be very reticent about the way they achieve it. Porting must be smoothly profiled, free of obstructions, and designed to pass gas through it at an optimum velocity. In the bad old days, far too much gas was passed, too slowly.

To increase gas flow, engines sometimes have what is known as forced induction, of two types – supercharging or turbocharging. In simple terms, a supercharger is a compressor (an air pump) driven directly from the engine's crankshaft. A turbocharger also has a compressor, but this is driven by a turbine activated by the exhaust gases from the engine. In many ways, therefore, a turbocharger produces 'power for free', and absolute ratings can be the highest of all.

Efficient combustion requires efficient mixing of fuel with the air. Carburettors are simple and effective, but a fuel injection system, in which carefully-timed, high-pressure jets of fuel are produced at the right place, is better still.

Different fuels have different potential, but here the cost element is important, as is the question of limiting pollution. Fuels with an octane rating of more than 100bhp would be best, but this either means using lead additives or using extremely expensive components of the refined oil from which all petrols are produced. 'Rocket fuel', which contains its own oxygen, has been tried on short-life race engines, but is impractical for road engine use. In any case it is banned from many applications.

Last, but by no means least, there is the question of engine revolving speeds. Without going into engineering formulae, it is enough to say that an engine produces more power if it can be made to revolve. If the same combustion efficiency is maintained at – say – 4000rpm as at 8000rpm, then the engine will produce twice as much power at the higher speed.

Modern engines, therefore, tend to have more, smaller cylinders than before, which means that the moving parts weigh less, and this allows them to be moved faster. For a given size of engine, a V12 will run faster, and will usually produce more power, than a V8.

Packing a punch into a limited
package – this was Ferrari's way of
mounting a four-cam vee-8,
transversely, with transmission and
final drive immediately behind it.

For the 1990s, it's fairly easy to guess at the engine for-
mations chosen for the *World's Most Powerful Cars*. They will
have between 8 and 16 cylinders (though V8s and V12s will
probably predominate). They will have twin overhead camshafts per cylinder head and at least four valves per cylinder.
They will certainly have fuel injection, perhaps with nozzles
firing direct into the cylinder heads. They may have forced
induction, and if so this will be provided by turbocharging.
Amazingly, they will rev faster, consume less fuel, and produce cleaner exhaust than ever before.

ABOVE
Most manufacturers agree that the
vee-formation engine is the most
compact; Alfa Romeo, with its vee-
6, is a very good example.

AC Cobra 289 and 427

PRODUCTION SPAN
1962 – 1968

ENGINE
V8–cyl, ohv

CAPACITY
260CID (4260cc), 289CID (4727cc), 427CID (6988cc)

MAXIMUM POWER
164, 195 and 345bhp

CHASSIS SUSPENSION
Tubular chassis frame, transverse leaf spring (later coil spring)/wishbone ifs and irs

BODY STYLE
2–door, 2–seater, open sports car

TOP SPEED
289CID: 138mph (221kmh); 427CID: 143mph (229kmh)

0–60mph
289CID: 5.5sec; 427CID: 4.8sec

The Cobra was a successful amalgam of British and American enterprise, for the engine and transmission were pure Detroit, while the rest of the structure was from AC of Thames Ditton, near London. The inspiration behind the Cobra came from the American ex-racing driver Carroll Shelby, though detail design and construction was carried out by AC.

In Britain and Europe the car was always called an AC, while in North America the cars tended to be called Shelby Cobras. Because the engines were provided by Ford, some people called them Ford Cobras too. When Carroll Shelby proposed mating Ford V8 engines to an AC chassis, AC was delighted, because its own 6-cylinder Ace was coming to the end of a successful career, and the car, called Cobra, took over for the next six years.

The secret of the new car's appeal was its powerful and torquey Ford-USA V8 engine. In standard form it was by no means highly-tuned, but race-prepared Cobras were phenomenally fast.

The deal was perfect. AC built the cars up to a certain point, then shipped them to California, where Shelby American added the engines and gearboxes. The result

BELOW
Traditional interior, and a big steering wheel, show that the AC Cobra was a real man's car. Everything was functional – glitz was for wimps . . .

was a car which looked good and had an enormous amount of character. If ever a car was exactly right for the 1960s, this was it.

The first few cars had 260-CID engines, but 289-CID engines were soon standardized, and the Cobra legend began to mount. Here was a light car that looked as if there might be some Ferrari heritage in it (some 1950s Ferraris looked quite similar, after all); it had tyre-stripping acceleration, a bellowing, all-American character, yet the engine and transmission could be fettled by any Ford-USA dealer.

The Cobra 289 was very fast, but the Cobra 427 which followed was phenomenal. In place of the 'small-block' Ford, AC inserted a 'big block' Ford V8, already a successful NASCAR-winning lump, used in the GT40 Mk II race cars. Well over 450bhp was available if the right tune-up kit was added – so that the Cobra 427 could beat any other car in the charisma stakes.

Just 560 Cobra 289s and 540 Cobra 427s were built, and in the 1980s the value of the surviving cars soared. A series of replicas and look-alikes were produced, and trademark disputes followed – such is the price of fame!

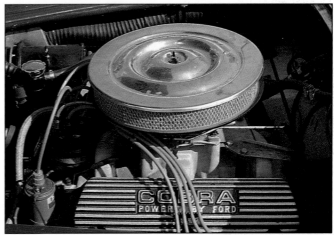

TOP
The Cobra's style was chunky, no-nonsense, but seductive in its own way. Under that curvaceous style was a massively powerful Ford vee-8 engine, which provided tyre-stripping performance.

ABOVE
Cobra power was by courtesy of Ford. Like this car, most had 289CID/4.7-litre vee-8 engines, but the most aggressive Cobras of all had the 345bhp 'big block' 427CID/7.0-litre vee-8 engine instead.

RIGHT
The AC badge on the British-market Cobra reminded everyone of the car's heritage.

BELOW
The Cobra, in side-view, was a purposeful-looking two-seater, with a long nose concealing the Ford-USA engine. Bumpers, fitted at front and rear, were more for decoration than for function.

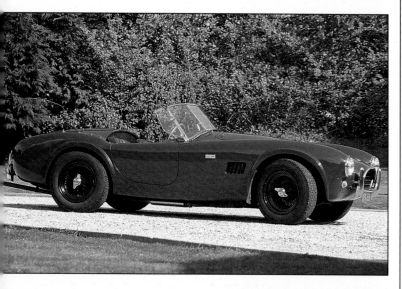

RIGHT
'Four on the floor' for the Cobra, with a T-bar which had to be lifted to allow engagement of reverse gear.

BELOW
In the 1960s Ford-USA was proud of its high-efficiency vee-8 engines, as this special rocker cover 'Powered by Ford' makes clear.

A B O V E
The Cobra looked impressive from
any angle, particularly from three-
quarter rear where the wide wheels
and the squat stance are obvious.
Under the skin there was a tubular
chassis, all-independent suspension,
four-wheel disc brakes, and the
promise of colossal acceleration.

Aston Martin Vantage and Vantage Zagato

PRODUCTION SPAN
1977 – 1989

ENGINE
V8–cyl, 2 ohc

CAPACITY
326CID (5340cc)

MAXIMUM POWER
300–432bhp

CHASSIS SUSPENSION
Platform chassis frame, coil spring/
wishbone ifs, coil spring/De Dion
rear suspension

BODY STYLE
2–door, 4–seater coupé or convertible

TOP SPEED
Vantage 170mph (273kmh); Vantage
Zagato approx 185mph (297kmh)

0–60mph
Vantage 5.5 sec, Vantage Zagato about
5.0 sec

A B O V E
The Vantage shared the same basic
body style as the other vee-8-
engined Aston Martins, but had a
blanked off radiator grille. The
bonnet hid a 432bhp vee-8 engine.

R I G H T
All that was best in British
craftsmanship went into the layout
and the construction of the Aston
Martin's fascia and instrument panel.

If Britain's Aston Martin concern built cars in Italy it would certainly be seen as a rival to Ferrari, for its post-war cars have always been very fast, very beautiful, and built in small numbers. However, it never managed to establish true 'supercar' status, even in the 1970s and 1980s when it produced a supremely powerful engine, and it came perilously close to bankruptcy at times.

A new Aston Martin chassis, complete with De Dion rear suspension, was launched in 1967, and an advanced, alloy V8 engine was revealed two years later. The chassis was to remain in production for more than 20 years, while the engine, in modified form, was chosen for Aston Martin's 1990s models too.

Although Aston Martin was convinced that its 4-cam V8 was one of the most powerful in the world, it was disgusted by the over-optimistic claims put out by some of its rivals, and refused to publish peak power figures for some years. It was not until West German legislation required publication that we learned just how good the engine had always been.

In 1977 the existing V8 model was 'up-gunned', with a considerably more powerful engine, given extra aero-

dynamic aids, and became the Vantage. In spite of the bluff coupé style, and the vast bulk of the machine, this had a top speed of around 170mph. In the mid-1980s, the coupé was joined by a lushly-furnished and equipped 'Volante' (convertible) version of the same style. Along the way the Vantage engine, originally fitted with four twin-choke Weber carburettors, was given Bosch fuel injection.

The Zagato derivative also followed in the mid-1980s, using the same rolling chassis as that of the Vantage, but equipped with a lumpy (some called it ungainly) coupé style by the Italian coachbuilder Zagato. This car was about 350lb (159kg) lighter than the Vantage, and had a lowered bonnet line, which meant that the induction side of the engine had to be fitted under an unsightly bonnet bulge.

Here, no question, was a phenomenally fast and powerful car (the quoted 432bhp was a minimum figure, probably surpassed only by the 12-cylinder Ferrari and Lamborghini 'supercars' of the day), which could reach 185mph (297kmh), and had colossal acceleration.

Several hundred Vantages were produced, but only 52 Zagatos (and 25 slightly lower-powered Zagato convertibles) followed it.

BELOW
The original vee-8-engined Aston Martin was launched in 1969, and cars of that type were built for twenty years. All the original cars were coupés, but the convertible followed in the 1980s. All the cars were hand-crafted, very carefully constructed, and fitted out with high-quality leather trim and seating.

BELOW
By the 1980s Aston Martin's shape had been modified to include a 'bustle' – a spoiler across the tail. The fat tyres, and the twin exhaust pipes, give a hint of the car's performance.

ABOVE
The Aston Martin's seating area was as much 'gentleman's club' as 1980s supercar, with the generous use of wood and padded leather. This was the Zagato-bodied version of the mid-1980s.

RIGHT
The famous badge on standard cars

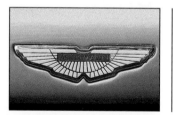

LEFT
. . . only slightly modified when Zagato built the bodies.

BELOW
The Zagato-bodied Aston Martin was lighter and more compact than the original British type, but had controversial styling, with a large bonnet bulge covering the engine.

LEFT
The Aston Martin Zagato was a
limited-production car based on the
familiar Vantage chassis. By any
standards it was an aggressive
shape, with vestiges of the old Aston
Martin grille style linked to new
headlamp details. The bonnet bulge
and the fresh air ducting can just be
seen.

BELOW
One unique feature of the Zagato-
bodied Aston Martin was the
restricted drop-glass area in the
doors.

Aston Martin Virage

PRODUCTION SPAN
Introduced in 1988/1989

ENGINE
V8–cyl, 2 ohc

CAPACITY
326CID (5340cc)

MAXIMUM POWER
335bhp

CHASSIS SUSPENSION
Steel chassis frame, coil spring/
wishbone ifs, coil spring/De Dion rear
suspension

BODY STYLE
2–door, 4–seater coupé

TOP SPEED
155mph (249kmh)

0–60mph
6.0 sec

Big, brawny, sleek, but
unmistakeably an Aston Martin, the
Virage was revealed in 1988, and
went into production a year later. It
was expected to be on sale until the
21st century.

Because of Aston Martin's recurring financial problems, there was never enough money available to invest in a new model. Ford-UK then appeared, as saviours, in 1987, and the future was under-pinned. A new car, called Virage, was previewed in 1988, with sales beginning towards the end of 1989.

In general layout, though not detail, the new Virage was like that of the old V8, which it replaced. There was a conventional steel chassis, the engine was front-mounted, driving the rear wheels, while the sleek new coupé style surrounded a compact 4-seater cabin.

The V8 engine was a much-modified version of the original design, for it had been given 4-valve cylinder heads (produced with the help of Callaway of Connecticut, USA), which allowed it to run on lead-free fuel, and to meet exhaust emissions requirements all round the world. Even so, it produced 330bhp – which was 25bhp more than the old 2-valve type.

The rest of the chassis was conventional by Aston Martin standards – a choice of 5-speed manual or 3-speed GM automatic transmissions, coil spring independent front suspension, and a newly-detailed De Dion rear end.

The principal novelty was in the style, which was a smoothly shaped coupé by the fashionable British duo of John Heffernan and Ken Greenley. The drag coefficient was in the 0.33–0.35 range, and although it looked smaller than the old V8 type it was actually longer and wider.

Although Aston Martin was now owned by Ford, there were no Ford parts in the new car. Ford, however, persuaded Bosch to help engineer anti-lock brakes for it, and these were slated to be added to 1990s models.

Although the Virage was by no means the most powerful car of its type, it was engineered to be environmentally friendly, and to meet any legislation, anywhere in the world. For that reason Aston Martin was confident that it would sell to the limit of the Newport Pagnell factory's capacity. Like the old V8 model, it was a big car, but with good, well-balanced road manners, a great deal of refinement, and that undeniable blend of British 'olde worlde' equipment, and high build quality for which an Aston Martin has always been famous.

Bentley 8-litre

PRODUCTION SPAN
1930–1931

ENGINE
6–cyl, ohc

CAPACITY
487CID (7983cc)

MAXIMUM POWER
Approx 200bhp

CHASSIS SUSPENSION
Steel chassis frame, leaf spring/beam axle front and rear suspension

BODY STYLE
Various – 2-door or 4-door, 5-seater saloons or tourers

TOP SPEED
101mph (162kmh)

0–60mph
Not measured

BELOW
Although the 8-litre Bentley was a very large car, it was usually equipped with very dignified body styles. This 4-door sports saloon was capable of 100mph, an outstanding achievement for 1930 when the car was unveiled.

OPPOSITE
The noble prow of this H. J. Mulliner bodied Bentley 8-litre was as famous, in its day, as the nose of a Ferrari or a Porsche would be today. The radiator needed to be very tall, because the engine itself was massive and powerful.

By any standards the last of the 'WO' Bentleys was a massive and impressive car. It was no wonder that detractors of these fine British cars derided them as the 'fastest lorries in the world'.

WO Bentley, who had trained as an apprentice in a railway workshop, and who had already designed successful aircraft engines, turned to motor car manufacture after the First World War. The company was always under-financed, and went through several sets of capital between 1919 and 1931, before it finally went into liquidation. Rolls-Royce then took over the Bentley name, and all subsequent Bentley models were really modified and more sporting Rolls-Royces.

Almost all 'WO' Bentleys had the same chassis layout and basic type of overhead-camshaft engines, with four-valve cylinder heads, and very small bore/long stroke dimensions. The original Bentley was a 3-litre model, with a 4-cylinder engine, but the 4½-litre 6-cylinder type followed in 1925, and this was enlarged to a massive 8-litre size in 1930.

The advanced engineering was backed by an extensive, and very successful racing programme, including five victories in the famous Le Mans 24-hour race, the last three being by 6-cylinder-engined cars.

Although the 8-litre had a large, heavy, and strictly conventional chassis, its 6-cylinder engine was a powerful and reliable monument to Bentley's far-sighted design of 1919. It was very large and heavy, but because it had 4-valve breathing it was very powerful by the standards of the day.

The cylinder head was integral with the cylinder block, though there was a separate light-alloy crankcase. The siâgle overhead camshaft was driven by a series of eccentrics and connecting rods at the front of the engine – these were

unfamiliar to motor car enthusiasts, though railway engineers would immediately see the derivation!

Behind the engine there was a 4-speed gearbox (but without synchromesh – this was strictly a General Motors phenomenon of the day) – the axle looked solid enough to drive a truck, and the big, finned, drum brakes were actuated by a mechanical linkage. Both the gear lever and the handbrake lever were mounted on the right of the (right-hand) driver's seat.

Even though the 8-litre weighed no less than 5400lb (2449kg) – this was what Cadillacs weighed in at in the 1960s – it was a very fast car, with huge torque developed from very low engine speeds. The car had a 100mph (160kmh) top speed (which was extremely rare for the early 1930s), and the coachbuilt bodies were beautifully built.

Rolls-Royce was apparently very worried about the 8-litre's impact on sales of its own Phantom II models, which were slower and no better built. The Derby company was relieved when the trade depression killed off Bentley – and the 8-litre model was never revived by the new management.

RIGHT
To own an 8-litre Bentley like this, in 1931, a sportsman had to be very rich, for such cars were very expensive to buy, had to be serviced every 1,000 miles or so, and needed the attention of a skilled mechanic to extract the best from their running gear.

LEFT
The vast 8-litre Bentley engine was a six-cylinder unit, with single overhead camshaft valve gear and four valves per cylinder. Note the magneto ignition, and the twin SU carburettors with minimal cleaning and silencing.

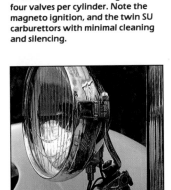

ABOVE
Headlamp mounting detail of the 8-litre Bentley. The extra driving lamp was added in the 1950s.

RIGHT
Comfort and dignity at up to 100mph was one of the unbeatable virtues of the Mulliner-bodied 8-litre Bentley.

Bentley Turbo R

PRODUCTION SPAN
Introduced in 1985

ENGINE
V8–cyl, ohv

CAPACITY
412CID (6750cc)

MAXIMUM POWER
330bhp

CHASSIS SUSPENSION
Unit-construction steel body/chassis structure, coil spring/wishbone ifs, coil spring/semi-trailing arm irs, with self-levelling control

BODY STYLE
4–door, 5-seater saloon

TOP SPEED
143mph (230kmh)

0–60mph
6.5 sec

RIGHT
Although the Turbo R was a 143-mph car, Bentley made absolutely no concessions to gain that sort of performance. Using the same basic body structure, style, and equipment as the Rolls-Royce Silver Spirit, the Turbo R also had sophisticated air conditioning, all-independent suspension with self-levelling, four-wheel disc brakes with full power assistance, automatic transmission – and it was built very slowly, very carefully, subjected to several road tests before delivery.

BELOW
The Bentley Turbo R was a heavy, but extremely fast saloon car, combining the very best Rolls-Royce features of quality and detail specification with a very powerful (330bhp) engine. The use of a painted grille surround was an easy recognition point.

Rolls-Royce took over Bentley in 1931, and by the 1950s Bentley models were little more than re-badged Rolls-Royce cars with a different grille and badging. By the end of the 1970s Bentley sales had fallen away dramatically.

In the 1980s the Bentley marque was progressively revived. Although the 1980s Bentleys were still obviously derived from Rolls-Royce cars, they became more sporty, mechanically different, and were aimed at the faster driver.

Rolls-Royce had introduced its V8 engine in 1959 and its first monocoque structure with advanced chassis engineering in 1965. The Silver Spirit model (also badged as a Bentley Mulsanne) of 1980 was an updated and re-styled statement of that design. At that time the 412CID/6.75-litre engine produced about 200bhp, though Rolls-Royce never revealed that figure.

The first turbocharged Bentley was the Mulsanne Turbo, appearing in 1982. Based closely on the conventional Mulsanne saloon, it combined a large Garrett Airesearch turbocharger with a 4-barrel Solex carburettor, and produced an (undisclosed) 298bhp. This was enough to give the bulky car a 135mph (217kmh) top speed, but the ride and roadholding were far too soft to make it a sports saloon.

From 1985 the car was updated to 'Turbo R' specification, with firmer and altogether better balanced handling, and with wider tyres and alloy wheels. Then, from the end of 1986, the car was given Bosch fuel injection for all markets, which helped boost the power to about 330bhp, and together with anti-lock braking this made the Turbo R into a big, heavy, but viable sporting machine.

By British standards it was, of course, a very large and thirsty machine, for it turned the scales at around 5300lb (2400kg), and usually returned around 14mpg (Imperial) fuel economy. On the other hand, the combination of Porsche-like acceleration with Rolls-Royce built quality, not forgetting the five or even 6-seater accommodation, was very attractive to a few hundred wealthy buyers every year It was a car which astonished by its contrasts. The engine was at once powerful and docile, the car was heavy but agile, and it felt sporty but was immensely refined and dignified. Few other European cars, except perhaps the latest multi-valve devices from West Germany, offered so much.

BMW M1

PRODUCTION SPAN
1978–1981

ENGINE
6–cyl, 2 ohc

CAPACITY
211CID (3453cc)

MAXIMUM POWER
277bhp

CHASSIS SUSPENSION
Separate steel chassis frame, coil
spring/wishbone ifs, coil spring/
wishbone irs

BODY STYLE
2–door, 2-seater coupé

TOP SPEED
162mph (260kmh)

0–60mph
5.5 sec

ABOVE
The beautiful M1 was originally
designed for BMW by Lamborghini,
but the production cars were
eventually built by Baur in West
Germany. Ak11 had left-hand-drive,
and the 24-valve six-cylinder engine
was mounted behind the cabin.

In the 1960s and 1970s BMW reinforced its reputation for advanced cars by winning many races at touring car level, and by developing successful engines for single-seater racing. In the 1970s it turned its attention to sports car racing, with the M1 project.

At the time, to compete head on with some Porsche models, BMW decided to compete in 'Group 4' racing. To qualify for this category BMW had to build 400 identical cars. BMW, more used to building thousands of cars in a week than 400 in a total run, decided to farm out this project, originally contracting Lamborghini to design, develop and manufacture the cars.

In the event Lamborghini's finances tottered, and they lost the contract. The result was that Marchesi of Italy built the frames, the Ital Design-styled shell (which was made of glass-fibre) was built by another Italian concern, but final assembly was bu Baur in West Germany.

The M1 (this means ('mid-Engined, Series 1') model had a mid-engined layout, with rear wheel drive, and while the engine was a further development of BMW's long-serving straight 6-cylinder unit, it was all-new in detail. The 3.5-litre size had already been seen on various production cars, but the twin overhead camshaft layout, complete with four valves per cylinder, was new, and in design terms was an obvious descendant of the already-famous Formula 2 (later Formula 1) 4-cylinder unit.

The racing project was abandoned even before the car went into serious production (a series of Procar races, as side-shows to the 1979 and 1980 Grand Prix races, were more 'show-business' than serious racing), which left the M1 as an exclusive road car. In all, 450 such cars were built, many of which went straight into private 'collections' and have rarely been used on the public highway.

But what a road car! In every way, except that it did not have a 12-cylinder engine and was a little less powerful, the M1 was a direct rival for cars like the Ferrari Boxer. Its mid-engine chassis was beautifully developed and superlatively balanced, while the whole car was carefully built and nicely detailed. Not many cars of this type had proper air conditioning and the familiar Teutonic attention to detail.

Its engine, complete with Bosch fuel injection, was at once docile and very broad-shouldered, and in full race form was capable of producing up to 500bhp. Indeed it was such a superb unit that it was used on later BMW road cars like the M6 and M5 models.

LEFT
Even though the M1 was a very limited-production machine, it was carefully developed by the Bavarian concern, and carried 'corporate' M- Sport badging.

BMW 850i V12

PRODUCTION SPAN
Introduced in 1989

ENGINE
V12-cyl, ohc

CAPACITY
305CID (4988cc)

MAXIMUM POWER
300bhp

CHASSIS SUSPENSION
Unit-construction steel body/chassis structure, coil spring/MacPherson strut ifs, coil spring/multi-link irs

BODY STYLE
2–door, 4-seater coupé

TOP SPEED
155mph (249kmh)

0–60mph
7.0 sec

BMW's new 850i V12 was launched in 1989, the first sporting coupé from Munich to feature the 305CID/5.0-litre vee-12 engine which had already been fitted to the latest big BMW saloons. Like its predecessors, it was a compact four-seater, and there was so much power that the top speed was artificially limited to 155mph.

Almost as soon as it regained financial stability in the 1960s, BMW added a coupé to its model range. In 1989 the long and successful life of the second-generation car came to an end, and a new 8-Series coupé was launched.

The 8-Series, like other BMW coupés before it, had a unique body style, but picked up its running gear from other BMW family cars. In this case the engine was a mighty V12 unit, recently put on sale in the 750i saloon, as was the transmission, while the suspension was a mixture of units from that car, and a brand new rear suspension intended for other BMW models to use in the 1990s.

The new 8-Series car, like its predecessors, had its engine up front, driving the rear wheels, and featured a

close-coupled 4-seater layout. At first there was only a closed coupé style, though a convertible version was widely forecast for launch in the early 1990s.

As with all such modern cars, it had a very 'slippery' shape, and the car could probably have reached speeds of well over 170mph (273kmh) if BMW had not voluntarily governed maximum speeds to around 155mph (249kmh) by electronic means.

The V12 engine was the first such unit to be put on sale by BMW, and was a design masterpiece, in technical detail, looks and construction. Even so, as specified for the 850i, it was only at the beginning of its development, for it had only a single overhead camshaft per cylinder bank.

However, even though it had two valves per cylinder, and was tuned more for docility, reliability and environment cleanliness, it still produced a very reliable 300bhp. Further developments of the design, some with twin overhead camshafts and 4-valve heads, were slated for use on other BMW models of the 1990s.

The 8-Series model and the engine which powered it were superbly detailed, in a manner possible from only a handful of European concerns. In leisurely use the engine was almost entirely inaudible, ultra-smooth and totally free of any temperament. Even so, the engine spun happily up to 5500rpm and beyond, giving just a hint of its awesome potential.

Bugatti Royale

PRODUCTION SPAN
1927–1933

ENGINE
8-cyl, ohc

CAPACITY
779CID (12763cc)

MAXIMUM POWER
300bhp

CHASSIS SUSPENSION
Separate steel chassis frame, leaf spring/beam axle front suspension, twin quarter-elliptic leaf spring/beam axle rear suspension

BODY STYLE
Various – six cars built

TOP SPEED
100mph (160kmh)

0–60mph
Not measured

This car looked magnificent and was boldly specified, but it was a complete sales failure. Bugatti of France designed the Type 41 or 'golden Bugatti' as an unsurpassed carriage, as a 'car for kings'. However even though it was called the Royale, and Ettore Bugatti made sure that it got a great deal of advance publicity, it was almost unsaleable.

In every way the Royale was the biggest, if not actually the best. It was the longest, the most powerful and the heaviest private car so far built. Its engine was originally intended for use in aircraft, and weighed as much as the average small car of the day. In most respects this was the wrong car, of the wrong type, produced at the wrong time.

Although members of the nobility inspected the car, none bought one. In the end only three private sales were achieved in six years – one each in France, Germany and the UK – and three other cars were built, and used, by members of the Bugatti family. Various coachbuilt bodies were used on various chassis (more than one car has been rebodied) – all six have survived, and today they are virtually priceless.

The chassis was conventional, but ran on a monstrous 14ft 2in (4.3m) wheelbase, with the engine up front and the 3-speed gearbox mounted in unit with the back axle. Once the car was moving, the direct second gear could be engaged, with top so high that it was strictly for autoroute cruising.

The engine was a colossal straight-eight, with overhead valve gear, a single overhead camshaft and three valves

BELOW
Aerodynamics meant nothing to Ettore Bugatti in the 1920s, when the Royale was designed, but attention to detail, and sheer panache, was all-important. The mascot – an elephant – is unique to this particular car.

To get a feel for the scale of the magnificent Bugatti Royale, remember that it ran on a 14ft 2in/4.3 metre wheelbase, and that it weighed more than 5,600lb/2540kg. This was motoring on the grandest possible scale.

per cylinder. The prototype Royale used a 14.7-litre/897CID, but for production a somewhat smaller 12.7-litre/779CID size was chosen instead.

By any standards the Type 41 was the biggest, the heaviest and the most powerful car so far produced for commercial sale. By Bugatti standards it was not technically advanced – smaller Bugattis used similar technical layouts – merely bigger and grander, in all respects. There was, however, dry sump lubrication (this was a heritage from the original aircraft application), and the engine produced no less than 300bhp.

The problem was that the Royale was so heavy – an average unladen weight was 5600lb (2540kg) – and the engine so inefficient in its breathing, that the car's performance was not as high as one might have expected. All in all, it was an utterly impractical flight of Gallic fancy – but the world of motoring would have been poorer without it.

Cadillac Eldorado (front-wheel-drive)

PRODUCTION SPAN
1966–1971

ENGINE
V8-cyl, ohv

CAPACITY
429CID (7031cc), 472CID (7736cc),
500CID (8195cc)

MAXIMUM POWER
340, 375 and 400bhp

CHASSIS SUSPENSION
Separate steel chassis frame, torsion
bar/wishbone ifs, leaf spring/beam axle
rear suspension

BODY STYLE
2-door, 5-seater coupé or convertible

TOP SPEED
120mph (193kmh) approx

0–60mph
10.0 sec

The original front-wheel drive
Cadillac Eldorado went on sale in
1966, and was a long and shapely
four-seater car, with 340bhp vee-8
engine. In the next few years this
original style would become even
more flamboyant, while engines
gew larger and ever more powerful.
It was unmistakeably a Cadillac, but
also a very fast car.

Although the first Cadillac Eldorado was launched in 1953, the type introduced for 1967 was completely different from its predecessors. Not only was it a new and smart coupé style, but it also had front-wheel-drive. By the mid-1980s most American cars would have front-wheel-drive; in the mid-1960s, when the Eldorado and its sister car the Oldsmobile Toronado were designed, it was a real novelty.

For Cadillac, the front-drive Eldorado was a completely new concept, intended to take the type a full step clear of cars like the Ford Thunderbird, with which it was to compete. Like most American cars of the day, it was big and heavy, though its cabin was quite small. Original front-drive Eldorados ran on a 120in (304cm) wheelbase, which might be short by Cadillac standards, but was as long as a complete BMC Mini-Minor! A typical Eldorado weighed about 4600lb (2086kg).

As in the Toronado, the Eldorado's engine sat above the line of the front suspension, with Hy-Vo chain drive to the automatic transmission, which was alongside, and under, the engine. There was torsion bar front suspension, but because there was no drive to the rear wheels these were linked by a 'dead' axle and half-elliptic springs.

The V8 engine, at first, was a massive update of the corporate Cadillac design, which had been substantially new for 1963. It was a 429CID unit, producing 340bhp. Then, for 1968, an all-new 472CID V8 was introduced, an engine immediately enlarged to 400CID and no less than 400bhp (gross) for 1970.

All these engines were big, lazy, reliable and long lasting cast-iron V8s in the true North American tradition – in fact they were the largest, in displacement, on sale anywhere in the world. Cadillac used the same engines, in near identical tune, in all the models in its line-up, and they were equally at home in the Eldorado as in the stretched limousines.

The engines, of course, were outstanding by any standards, even though their quoted outputs were 'gross' – which means that they cannot be compared, directly, with European engines listed in 'nett' form.

They needed to be, of course. Cars like the Eldorado were heavy and poor aerodynamically, (aerodynamics were simply ignored) and their automatic transmissions were inefficient. It was no wonder that top speeds (where they could be achieved in a country riddled with speed limits) were limited, and fuel economy awful.

Nothing, however, could detract from the sheer muscle, allied to some refinement, of Cadillacs built in this period, for during the 1970s exhaust emission limitations saw the power ratings gradually reduced.

Chevrolet Corvette – 1960s

PRODUCTION SPAN
1960–1970

ENGINE
V8-cyl, ohv

CAPACITY
283, 327, 396, 427 and 454CID
(4,635, 5,355, 6,486,
6,994 and 7,436cc)

MAXIMUM POWER
315–460bhp

CHASSIS SUSPENSION
Separate steel chassis frame, coil spring/
wishbone ifs, leaf spring/beam axle rear
suspension to 1962, transverse leaf
spring/wishbone irs from 1963

BODY STYLE
2-door, 2-seater coupé or convertible

TOP SPEED
435bhp: 160mph (257kmh)

0–60mph
435bhp: 6.3 sec

ABOVE
Corvettes came in all shapes and
sizes – this was a four-headlamp
version of the second-generation
model, first seen in the late 1950s.

BELOW
By 1961 the second-generation
Corvette had matured, with four
headlamps and even more
decoration than when launched. This
red with cream colour scheme was
very popular, while the lift-off
hardtop was optional equipment.

The Corvette's career started slowly in 1953, when it was equipped with an old style 6-cylinder engine and automatic transmission. Things looked up when Chevrolet's first V8 was offered in 1955. By 1960 the Corvette had more power options and could be a really fast car.

Corvette performance was at its height in the 1960s. V8 engine options increased in power as the decade progressed, but from 1971 the new exhaust emissions laws led to a progressive de-tuning.

Although all Corvettes were 2-seater sports cars, with front-mounted engines and glass-fibre bodies, there were three different Corvette generations in the 1960s, several facelifts and a multitude of options. The famous Sting Ray style was launched for 1963, while the 'Mako Shark' style displaced it for 1968. Early '60s cars had a beam rear axle, but from 1963 there was independent rear suspension, with four-wheel disc brakes following for 1965.

There were two types of V8, both being Chevrolet-designed cast-iron overhead-valve units. The 'small-block' type, originally revealed in the mid-1950s, grew from 265CID in the 1955 model to 400CID in the late 1970s; in European terms that is 4.3 to 6.55 litres. It was a lightweight unit which, in highly-tuned form, was a free-revving unit used in many other cars, and in several types of motorsport.

In addition, there was the much larger 'large block' Chevrolet engine, first used in Corvettes of 1965, which started life at 396CID and was progressively enlarged to 454CID (6.5 to 7.4 litres). This was typical Detroit 'heavy-metal',

being physically much larger and heavier than the 'small-block' design, slower-revving, but bursting with steam-engine-like torque.

In both cases the power ratings looked better than they were, for they were quoted 'gross', before various in-car losses were taken into effect. Even so, the V8 powered Corvettes could, and often did, out-run imported sports cars costing several times as much, all with engines no more highly tuned than those used in other Chevrolet models.

Unless a Corvette was sadly neglected, its running gear lasted almost indefinitely, bringing really spine-tingling acceleration within the reach of the young, and the not-so-well-off, among America's drivers. Then, as later, the Corvette was the sports car which every American driver wanted to own.

LEFT
Although the Corvette was a fast and purposeful car, it was also styled to excite, even when standing still. This 1960 model has extra air scoops fitted behind the front wheels.

Chevrolet Corvette ZR-1

PRODUCTION SPAN
Introduced in 1989

ENGINE
V8-cyl, 2 ohc per bank

CAPACITY
350CID (5727cc)

MAXIMUM POWER
380bhp

CHASSIS SUSPENSION
Separate backbone chassis frame, leaf spring/wishbone ifs, leaf spring/radius arm irs

BODY STYLE
2-door, 2-seater coupé

TOP SPEED
180mph (289kmh)

0–60mph
5.6 sec

Chevrolet announced the new generation Corvette in 1983, a car which combined beauty and advanced engineering at amazingly competitive prices. There was a new backbone chassis frame with all independent suspension, and a sleek body style featuring a hatchback and a removable roof panel.

On the original production cars the standard engine was a 205bhp version of the latest 'small block' 350CID/5.7-litre V8, with fuel injection, but still with pushrod-operated overhead valve gear.

Soon after this GM absorbed the British Lotus concern, and set its designers to produce a magnificent engine especially for Corvette use. The result, unveiled in 1989, was the superb Corvette ZR-1, certainly the fastest Corvette yet built, and one of the fastest production sports cars in the world.

RIGHT
The mid-1980s Corvette style was launched in 1984, and still looked great in 1989 when the 380bhp ZR-1 version was introduced. Like all such Corvettes, this was a pure two-seater, with a front-mounted vee-8 engine, and a flamboyant character.

BOTTOM RIGHT
The ZR-1 looked as sleek, and as purposeful, as any Italian-styled supercar, but the shape was created by GM in Detroit.

BELOW
The ZR-1 Corvette, introduced in 1989, combined classic Corvette styling with advanced Lotus engineering technology. The top speed, where you could use it, was around 180mph.

The ZR-1 used all the well-proven elements of the mid-1980s Corvette, but improved them considerably. The engine was a beautifully detailed 350CID, all aluminium, and with new cylinder heads featuring twin overhead camshafts and four valves per cylinder producing a very genuine 380bhp (DIN) at 6000rpm. Although that sounds to be less than that of engines fitted to 1960s 'Vettes, the peak was measured in a different way. Without doubt, this was the most powerful Corvette so far produced.

In addition, for economy driving the engine effectively operated on only half of its valves, benefiting from an ingenious variable valve timing system.

Backing it was a massive 6-speed ZF gearbox, and the suspension had been reworked to make this a real 'super-car' package.

Although the ZR-1 had only rear-wheel-drive, its 275/40 section 17in (43cm) tyres, on 11in (28cm) rear rims, coped splendidly with all the brute power. Looking little different from the normal Corvette, the ZR-1 performed like a Ferrari or a Lamborghini, made all the right supercar noises, yet met all USA legislation, and was sold at prices ludicrously low by comparison.

Once the Italians suggested that Detroit could never even begin to approach their own standards of performance, handling, and technical sophistication. With the ZR-1 they had to think again. In the 1990s, who knows what may happen? The ZR-1 might overtake the Italians in prestige as well as in performance . . .

Chrysler 300 models

PRODUCTION SPAN
1955–1956

ENGINE
V8-cyl, ohv

CAPACITY
331, 354, 392 and 413CID
(5,422, 5,799, 6,421
and 6,765cc)

MAXIMUM POWER
300–405bhp

CHASSIS SUSPENSION
Separate steel chassis frame (later unit construction), coil springs, later torsion bar/wishbone ifs, leaf spring/beam axle rear suspension

BODY STYLE
2-door, 5-seater coupé and convertible

TOP SPEED
300E: 125mph (200kmh)

0–60mph
300E: 8.5 sec

ABOVE
This was a 1956 Chrysler 300B, showing off the two-door five-seater coupé layout, which was powered by a 300bhp 'Hemi' engine.

RIGHT
The Chrysler 300B of 1956 was a big, heavy, but very fast car, built only in limited numbers, but able to beat any other American car of its day.

Although Chrysler's 300 'Letter' models were based on the same chassis and suspension as other current Chrysler models, they were always equipped with the most powerful possible engines, and fitted with a series of individual coupé and convertible body styles.

The 'Letter' name comes because every model year Chrysler changed the model title. The original car was the 300, that sold in 1956 was the 300B, in 1957 it was the 300C, this continuing to 1965 and the model 300L when the prestigious range was dropped. Production was strictly limited – in 1958, for instance, only 809 cars were built, and in 1961 only 1617. Chrysler sold these at a premium price, with an 'exclusive' tag.

The chassis engineering was strictly conventional Detroit, complete with soft suspension, drum brakes, and beam axle rear suspension, but under the glossy bonnets there was a great deal of real V8-power – more than any other Chrysler model – and the shape of the cars was personally influenced by chief stylist Virgil Exner. All cars were 2-door closed coupés at first, but a convertible option became available for 1957.

At first the 300 'Letter' models were powered by Chrysler's excellent 'Hemi' V8 design, an engine which had hemispherical combustion chambers and cross-pushrod valve gear. Originally it was 331CID design, with 300bhp, but by 1958 and the 300D it had been pushed up to 392CID and 390bhp. Production economics then took their toll, for further 300 'Letter' models had slightly less power and conventional 'wedge-head' castings.

No other American carmaker, not even Cadillac, was offering as much power at this time, so the 300 'Letter' models were at the peak of Detroit's power pecking order.

Although these cars were always very powerful and splendidly equipped, they were also very heavy, which took the edge off the performance. In 1962, for instance, the 300H model had 413CID and 405bhp, but it weighed no less than 4000lb (1814kg) at the kerbside. That, and the convertible's price of $5,461 meant that only 558 cars were built in that model year.

Chrysler's 300s, in other words, were high performance flagships, rather than stripped-out tyre burners. They sold to the well heeled, rather than to the young show offs, which explains why they became collectors' items in later years.

ABOVE
This was the original Chrysler 300, as launched in 1955, as a two-door five-seater coupé. Some say that Volvo's Amazon style was inspired by the divided grille of the 300 range.

LEFT
By 1957 the Chrysler 300 family had advanced to 300C, with a sleeker body shell which included rear tail fins and . . .

BELOW
. . . four headlamps and a single piece grille.

Cizeta-Moroder V16T

PRODUCTION SPAN
Introduced in 1989

ENGINE
V16-cyl, 2 ohc per bank

CAPACITY
366CID (5995cc)

MAXIMUM POWER
560bhp

CHASSIS SUSPENSION
Separate steel chassis frame, coil springs/wishbone ifs, coil spring/wishbone irs

BODY STYLE
2-door, 2-seater coupé

TOP SPEED
204mph (326kmh)

0–60mph
4.5 sec

This magnificent mid-engined monster, complete with a transversely-mounted V16 engine, could have been designed only in Italy, where supercar engineering lurks around every corner and in every artisan's workshop.

The Cizeta was developed to beat the two other mid-engined Italian supercars – the Ferrari Testarossa and the Lamborghini Countach – and to do that it had to look even more startling, and have even more advanced running gear, and greater power.

The prototype was beautiful, and had a startling specification. Naturally everyone expected it to have a mid-mounted engine, but not something as complex as a 90-degree V16, and certainly not one that was mounted transversely, in unit with its transmission. The claimed top speed – 204mph (326kmh), if you could find anywhere to prove it – was ahead of any other car on sale at the time.

With styling by Marcello Gandini (who shaped the Countach in the 1970s), and with engineering by a group of ex-Lamborghini technicians, it was clear that the Cizeta project was serious. The new car was longer, wider and subtly smoother than the Countach – and the engine produced an extra 115bhp.

Apart from its looks, and that startling top-speed claim, the most impressive feature of the Cizeta was its engine. It was an all-alloy unit, with twin overhead camshafts per bank (eight in all, because drive was by chain from the centre of the crankshaft!), four valves per cylinder and two separate Bosch fuel injection systems.

By comparison, the Lamborghini's four-cam V12, with Weber carburettors, looked, and sounded, positively old fashioned.

Because it was a car which had to be driveable at town speeds, but had to reach for that 200mph-plus (320kmh) top speed, it was high geared, and was obviously happier out on the Italian autostrada than in a traffic jam. Even so, it had well-weighted, power-assisted steering, and its creator Claudio Zampolli insisted that it would also have air-conditioning good enough to keep a millionaire cool in the Arizona desert.

More than anything, however, it had a sensational engine layout, the like of which had never been seen before. No more than 25 Cizetas were built in the first production year, and after inspecting the complexities of the V16 engine one could see why. Nothing quite as exciting had been launched since Cadillac's own V16 appeared in 1930.

For the connoisseur of Italian styling, there was no mistaking the hand of Marcello Gandini in the shape of the fabulous vee-16 engined Cizeta Moroder. The engine was behind the cabin, and transversely mounted.

Dodge Charger Daytona, and Plymouth Superbird

PRODUCTION SPAN
1969 and 1970

ENGINE
V8-cyl, ohv

CAPACITY
426CID (6977cc)

MAXIMUM POWER
425bhp

CHASSIS SUSPENSION
Unit construction steel structure, torsion bar/wishbone ifs, leaf spring/beam axle rear suspension

BODY STYLE
2-door, 5-seater coupé

TOP SPEED
135mph (217kmh) approx

0–60mph
7.5 sec

In 1969 and 1970 the Chrysler Corporation built two near identical cars, specifically to meet the latest NASCAR racing rules. NASCAR racing favoured cars with an excellent aerodynamic shape (for this allowed high speeds on the fast over tracks), but demanded a certain minimum number of cars to be produced in each year.

Chrysler set out to beat the system. In 1969 NASCAR demanded 500 cars, so a series of 505 Dodge Charger Daytonas were produced. A year later NASCAR changed the rules, to require 1500 cars – so 1920 near identical Plymouth Road Runner Superbirds were built. The cars were wildly successful – in 1970 they won no fewer than 38 of the 48 major races! Although utterly impractical as road machines, the Chrysler twins did their job on the tracks.

The cars were based on the shared body cell and running gear of the current Dodge Charger/Plymouth Road Runner coupés, but they were given long 'bullet' noses and towering rear-deck spoilers, or aerofoils. The intention was to provide real downforce at high speeds and to lower the drag characteristics.

The result was so successful that NASCAR changed the rules yet again at the end of 1970, and banned the beaky-

RIGHT
Well-engineered race cars never disappoint, even in the study of tiny details.

BELOW
To make the Superbird and its sister car (the Dodge Charger Daytona) even faster, Chrysler added a long wedge nose, and a high-mounted tail spoiler. Both improved the aerodynamics and trimmed the handling.

To make a fast car even faster,
Chrysler added a longer nose and . . .

. . . a vast rear tail spoiler to the
cabin of its four-seater Charger and
Roadrunner muscle cars. In the 1969
and 1970 these beaky-nosed
'homologation specials' were almost
unbeatable in NASCAR racing.

nosed Mopar monsters from the tracks. Chrysler didn't mind – the point had been made.

Although some cars were built with Chrysler's conventional 440CID/390bhp V8 and TorqueFlite automatic transmission, the top of the range option, which was specified by all true enthusiasts, was the famous 426CID/7.0-litre V8 'Hemi' engine, which offered no less than 425bhp, and drew on all the racing experience gained by Mopar products in the previous decade and more.

Thus equipped, the Daytona/Superbird (the names mattered little, as the two cars were near identical twins) was an amazingly powerful machine, which was so far 'over the top' in styling for road car use that it was almost laughable. Anyone who took one into heavy commuter traffic risked not only boiling the engine in snarl-ups, but damaging the long nose (which was a long way ahead of the front wheels, and could not be seen from the driving seat), and having the lofty rear aerofoil damaged by hooligans.

No matter. It drove a huge hole through NASCAR'S racing regulations, brought huge amounts of publicity to the Chrysler Corporation, and proved, yet again, that the Hemi engine was perhaps the best in the world.

LEFT
The Road Runner Superbird took its badge from the well-known cartoon character which could never be captured.

RIGHT
The best of the best be-winged Mopar monsters had the famous Chrysler 'hemi' engine under the bonnet. This was the unit which helped the Charger and Road Runner models to win so many races in a short career.

BELOW
Rakish car, Californian sunshine, the promise of enormous performance, and real exclusivity. What more could a Plymouth Superbird owner wish for in 1970, when this car was new?

Ferrari Superamerica and Superfast

PRODUCTION SPAN
1955–1960

ENGINE
V12-cyl, ohc

CAPACITY
303CID (4961cc)

MAXIMUM POWER
340 and 400bhp

CHASSIS SUSPENSION
Separate steel chassis frame, transverse leaf spring (Superfast, coil spring)/ wishbone ifs, leaf spring/beam axle rear suspension

BODY STYLE
2-door, 2-seater coupé, various styles

TOP SPEED
165mph (265kmh) approx

0–60mph
6.6 sec

Early in the 1950s Ferrari road cars were based around a simple chassis design and de-tuned versions of the company's original V12 engine. Then, from 1953 onwards, the Italian concern built a limited number of cars based around the 'Lampredi' large-block V12 engine, first used in Ferrari race cars at the beginning of the decade.

Except that the design of the front suspension was changed towards the end of the 1950s, the same basic 102in (259cm) wheelbase chassis was used throughout. Ferrari did not build its own bodies, but supplied rolling chassis to companies like Pininfarina and Boano for completion. The styling of the cars, therefore, was to the customers' tastes.

The first cars were called '342 America', having 250CID/ 4.1-litre engines, and the 375 America had an enlarged version of this unit. But the real powerhouses were the Superamerica/Superfast types, which used slightly de-tuned versions of the famous 303CID/4.96-litre V12 engines which Ferrari had used to win the Le Mans 24 Hour race in 1954.

In this form, the Superamerica had 340bhp (some cars were built with 4300bhp engines!), and when matched to a strong though unsophisticated 4-speed gearbox and a Sleek Pininfarina body style, it was enough to push the road car up to 165mph (265kmh).

This, without question, made the Superamerica the fastest road car in the world at this time, which meant that the cars were legendary even before they dropped out of production. The engine was a 60 degree V12 unit, hand crafted by Ferrari, and was fitted with three downdraught dual-choke Weber carburettors. Not only was it extremely powerful, it was also a fine piece of engineering sculpture, which was almost totally reliable if regularly and diligently maintained.

Such Ferraris, of course, were extremely expensive to buy and maintain, but they repaid their owners with great charisma and 'presence'. Then, as in later years, there was nothing quite as exciting to the enthusiast as the sight of a Ferrari coupé, allied to the splendid noise of the V12 engine.

These cars were unmatched for performance by any other road machine of the 1950s – the Mercedes-Benz 300SL, for instance, did not come close.

Rarity value? In five years only 38 Model 410 Ferraris were produced.

Ferrari 365GTB/4 Daytona

PRODUCTION SPAN
1968–1974

ENGINE
V12-cyl, 2 ohc per bank

CAPACITY
238CID (4390cc)

MAXIMUM POWER
352bhp

CHASSIS SUSPENSION
Separate steel chassis frame, coil spring)/wishbone ifs, coil spring/ wishbone ifs

BODY STYLE
2-door, 2-seater coupé or convertible (Spider)

TOP SPEED
174mph (280kmh)

0–60mph
5.4 sec

Throughout the 1960s Ferrari's road cars became faster and faster. The 275GTB was the first to have the rear-gearbox/ independent-rear suspension chassis, the 275GTB/4 had the more powerful four-cam engine, and the Daytona – which took over in 1968 – was the most sensational front-engined Ferrari of all. The Daytona name was chosen to commemorate a great Ferrari race car victory at the Florida circuit.

According to authentic road test figures, the Daytona was the world's fastest road car at the time it was in production,

ABOVE
The beautiful Daytona was Ferrari's fastest ever front-engined car, and had a purposeful two-seater interior. The gearchange had a visible 'gate', while those seats were meant for serious motoring, not for lounging.

RIGHT
Not only was the Ferrari Daytona one of the world's fastest cars when introduced in 1968, but it was also one of the most beautiful. Styled by Pininfarina, it had a long sleek bonnet covering the four-cam vee-12 engine, and a two-seater cabin. All the best Ferraris, of course, were painted in this famous shade of red.

and it was some years before the mid-engined supercars of the 1980s managed to wrest that title away.

There were two reasons for this. One was that the shape of the two-seater car, which was styled by Pininfarina but manufactured by Scaglietti, was extremely efficient. The other was that the 238CID/4.4-litre V12 engine was one of the world's outstanding power units.

Some cars look as if they are doing 100mph (160kmh) even when standing still, and the Daytona was one of these. There will always be arguments, of course – was the closed coupé a more beautiful car than the open tourer or Spider? The coupé, of course, was the faster car, but in later years the open top version became more valuable as a 'classic' or 'investment' car.

Under the glossy skin (and all true Ferraris, of course, were painted Italian red!), the glorious V12 engine was mounted in the nose, driving the rear wheels through a rear-mounted 5-speed gearbox/final drive assembly. There was independent suspension all round, and the handling balance was superb. In every way, this was one of the most effective and versatile road cars of all time.

The engine was really the final flowering, the ultimate statement, of every Ferrari V12 unit so far made, and was distantly related to that used in the Superamerica models. Like all other such classic units, its main castings were in light alloy, and it had a 60-degree angle between banks. Each cylinder head had twin overhead camshafts, there

were two valves per cylinder, and the unit was topped by a row of six twin-choke Weber carburettors.

Like every Ferrari engine, it was at once powerful yet docile, reliable yet race-bred, smooth yet rorty. The Daytona could be driven slowly and gently without fuss, but it was happiest when being urged along, with the engine singing away between 5000 and 6000 rpm, and with the car dancing around on the sinewy roads of the French or Italian mountains.

The Daytona was a supreme car, not overshadowed by the mid-engined Berlinetta Boxer which displaced it. No wonder you will have to pay a king's ransom to buy one in the 1990s.

BELOW
Not a line out of place, not a spare inch of styling – the Daytona had been imitated, but never matched, in more recent years. It looked every inch of the 170mph Grand Tourer that it actually was.

Ferrari Berlinetta Boxer

PRODUCTION SPAN
1973 – 1984

ENGINE
Flat-12-cyl, 2 ohc per bank

CAPACITY
238CID (4390cc) and 302CID (4942cc)

MAXIMUM POWER
360 and 380bhp

CHASSIS SUSPENSION
Separate steel chassis frame, coil spring/wishbone ifs, coil spring/ wishbone irs

BODY STYLE
2-door, 2-seater coupé

TOP SPEED
4.4-litre model: 171mph (275kmh)

0–60mph
4.4-litre model: 6.5 sec

FAR RIGHT
The Boxer was almost a Ferrari racing car for the road, for it had almost every mechanical feature previously used on racing sports cars – flat-12 engine mounted behind the cockpit, all-independent suspension, huge brakes, Pininfarina styling, and a top speed of more than 170mph.

BELOW
Pininfarina's style for the Boxer was so carefully detailed that the mid-mounted engine position is not obvious. The Boxer went on sale in 1973, and still looked modern more than ten years later.

Lamborghini launched the mid-engined Miura in 1966, and Maserati followed up with the mid-engined Bora in 1971. It was inevitable that Ferrari would follow suit shortly. Five years after the remarkable Daytona had gone on sale, the equally amazing Berlinetta Boxer took over. Straightaway it became the car by which other concerns set their standards.

Ferrari's mid-engined contender in the supercar stakes was unique in several ways. There had been mid-engined 12-cylinder racing Ferraris before, but this was the Maranello concern's first such road machine. It was the first Ferrari road car to use a newly developed flat-12 engine, and this sat on top of (rather than ahead of), the transmission/final drive assembly.

Because of their layout, such engines are usually called 'Boxers', which explains why the new Ferrari's full title was 365GT4/BB, with the 'BB' standing for Berlinetta Boxer. For the whole of its long career, the car was called 'the Boxer'.

Except that the combined engine/transmission package looked too bulky and lofty to suit race car use, in many ways this was in fact a racing car for the road. It had an advanced chassis, its Pininfarina body style looked sleek, purposeful, and totally without unnecessary decoration,

and the 2-seater cabin was definitely angled towards the functional rather than the luxurious. There was a little luggage space in this mid-engined car, but any Boxer owner planning a long stay away from home was wise to send his bags on ahead, or in a 'tender' car!

Most cars seem to get more powerful and faster as their career progresses - but the Boxer did not. The original car had a highly-tuned 4.4-litre engine which produced 380bhp; from 1976 the car became 512BB, at which point the engine went up to 4.94 litres, but this was a more flexible, more environmentally friendly derivative, less powerful and more torquey than before. Top speeds actually fell from around 171mph (275kmh) to about 163mph (262kmh), to howls of disbelief from Ferrari fanatics.

To redress the balance Ferrari specified fuel injection (instead of massed Weber carburettors) from 1979, but this made little difference to the performance. Such top speeds, however, were rarely even investigated by Boxer owners, who continued to revel in the colossal acceleration, character, and charisma of their car.

It would need a very special car indeed to take over from the Boxer. The Testarossa was that car, and no one complained.

Ferrari
Testarossa

PRODUCTION SPAN
Introduced in 1984

ENGINE
Flat-12-cyl, 2 ohc per bank

CAPACITY
302CID (4942cc)

MAXIMUM POWER
390bhp

CHASSIS SUSPENSION
Separate steel chassis frame, coil spring/wishbone ifs, coil spring/ wishbone irs

BODY STYLE
2-door, 2-seater coupé

TOP SPEED
180mph (290kmh)

0–60mph
5.8 sec

Testarossa! Engineering by Ferrari, styling by Pininfarina. Need any more be said?

ABOVE
Room for two in the Testarossa's cabin, in great comfort, and surrounded by superbly detailed instruments and controls. To many people, this was heaven on wheels.

BELOW
The Testarossa's side strakes were decorative, but also helped to channel air into the engine bay.

By the early 1980s the existing mid-engined Ferrari super-car – the 512BBi Boxer – was due for replacement, but Ferrari did not see the need to produce a completely new design. Instead, for launch at the end of 1984, the Italian concern produced the Testarossa, which was effectively a completely re-worked chassis, clothed in a sexy new coupé style.

First and foremost, Ferrari had to tackle the question of performance. Whether or not a high top speed was of value to the customer was not important – this top-of-the-tree Ferrari had to be at least as fast as the main opposition, which was the Lamborghini Countach.

Ferrari therefore re-worked the flat-12 engine, retaining the 302CID/4.94-litre size, but giving it completely new cylinder heads, with four valves per cylinder. Ferrari painted the heads in red crackle paint, and since the Italian for 'redhead' is 'testarossa', this provided the excuse for reviving the name of a famous late 1950s Ferrari racing sports car.

Compared with the last of the Boxers, the power leapt back up to 390bhp, there was even more torque than before, and the result was a car with a top speed of at least 180mph (290kmh). Honour was satisfied.

The old Boxer's chassis and mechanical layout was mostly retained, except that the front cooling radiator was discarded, in favour of two 'hip-mounted' radiators, alongside the engine bay, in true racing car fashion. At the same time the chassis settings were re-worked, and the new car was given

BELOW
Two discreet badges tell their own story on this Testarossa – Ferrari on the wheels, and Pininfarina on the body shell. Both promised impeccable character.

extra wide rear wheels, which had 10 in (25cm) rims.

To match this new chassis, Ferrari commissioned a sexy new body style from Pininfarina. Although the new car was no longer than before, it was considerably wider. There was also the opportunity to include very distinctive strakes along the doors and flanks, the better to channel fresh air into the cooling radiators.

The Testarossa looked so fast, and was so obviously well developed, and ready to be driven at ridiculously high speeds, that it almost sold itself. No one, not even with a million dollars, could walk into a showroom, off the street, and drive away in a Testarossa.

People without a soul looked at cars like the Testarossa, and asked why mere mortals needed cars with a top speed of 180mph (290kmh) in a speed-limited world. True driving enthusiasts didn't bother to answer, but merely enjoyed the 390bhp capability of the mid-engined Ferrari, and howled off into the distance. Wouldn't anyone?

LEFT
Opening a door was more than a chore on a Testarossa, for it also showed how the air-channeling strakes were fixed to the shell.

ABOVE
Not only was the Ferrari Testarossa's engine one of the most powerful in the world, but it *looked* incredibly powerful too. The layout was a flat-12, with four valves per cylinder.

Ferrari 288GTO

PRODUCTION SPAN
1984 – 1986

ENGINE
V8-cyl, 2 ohc

CAPACITY
174CID (2855cc)

MAXIMUM POWER
400bhp

CHASSIS SUSPENSION
Separate steel chassis, coil spring/
wishbone ifs, coil spring/wishbone irs

BODY STYLE
2-door, 2-seater coupé

TOP SPEED
189mph (304kmh)

0–60mph
4.9 sec

TOP RIGHT
The lines, of course, were pure Pininfarina/Ferrari, but the discreet 'GTO' badge on the tail, and the three-piece road wheels, told us that this was the 288GTO, and something very special.

ABOVE
The 288GTO looked similar to the 308GTB, but had a longer wheelbase, with its engine placed fore-and-aft instead of transversely. The style, by Pininfarina, was as purposeful as ever.

'GTO' is one of those titles made famous on both sides of the Atlantic. In Italy, as Gran Turismo Omologato it has been applied to two widely different Ferraris, while in the USA it was given to a mid-1960s Pontiac.

In Italy, 'GTO' means that a car was designed with motor sport in mind and that it has been approved (homologated or 'omologato' in Italian) by the authorities. In the 1960s Ferrari produced the front-engined 250GTO, a fine machine, but in the mid-1980s the 288GTO came along, a car which pushed out the already wide limits of Ferrari road-car performance.

The 288GTO's story started with the mid-engined 308GTB, the successful and long-running V8 engined Ferrari which combined Pininfarina styling and elegance with a pure bred chassis and running gear. In this application the engine was transversely mounted, behind the seats, and naturally there was all independent suspension and four massive disc brakes.

During its life, the four overhead-cam V8 engine first inherited fuel injection, then 4-valve cylinder heads, and was eventually enlarged to 3.2-litres. All this, however, was merely a prelude.

In 1984 Ferrari unveiled the 288GTO, a car which was developed from the 328GTB, but was different, faster, and more dramatic in so many ways. Compared with the GTB, the GTO's chassis had a slightly lengthened wheelbase, and the engine had been re-aligned, its crankshaft now along the line of the frame rather than across it. It needed a new gearbox, therefore, to drive the rear wheels.

The engine itself was reduced in size to 2855cc, but was equipped with twin turbochargers (one per cylinder bank). It produced a remarkable 400bhp DIN, more than any other Ferrari currently in production. That meant that it produced 140bhp/litre, as much and more than any other road car engine of the mid-1980s.

The result was a car which looked superficially like the existing GTB, for it had a two-door steel coupé body style, but one which was much more a 'racer' than a 'road' car.

It was built in strictly limited quantities, a policy which instantly made a GTO a 'collector's car'. Originally Ferrari said it would produce only 200, though in the end a total of 271 were built and racing driver Niki Lauda took delivery of the last one in 1987.

The GTO, in every way, was race proven, with excellent road manners. With a top speed of nearly 190mph (305kmh), it was the world's fastest car when launched, faster than the Testarossa, and Lamborghini's Countach. Not until the Porsche 959 went on sale was it beaten.

The GTO also looked sensational, and was the sort of car that any motoring fanatic would like to have tucked away in his garage.

LEFT
The Ferrari 288GTO was a beautiful and compact two-seater car, with 400bhp engine and 189mph top speed.

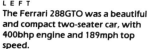

RIGHT
Head-on view of the Ferrari 288GTO of 1984–1986, a near-190 mph supercar built in very limited quantities. The 'prancing horse' is one of the world's most famous badges.

Ferrari F40

PRODUCTION SPAN
Introduced in 1987

ENGINE
V8-cyl, 2 ohc

CAPACITY
179CID (2936cc)

MAXIMUM POWER
478bhp

CHASSIS SUSPENSION
Separate steel chassis, coil spring/
wishbone ifs, coil spring/wishbone irs

BODY STYLE
2-door, 2-seater coupé

TOP SPEED
201mph (323kmh)

0–60mph
3.5 sec

RIGHT
F40 meant 'fortieth anniversary Ferrari', one of the world's fastest, most powerful *and* most desirable cars. With a claimed top speed of 201mph, it gave way to nobody.

LEFT
To the delight of all Ferrari enthusiasts, the F40 was built in considerable numbers. This mouth-watering shot shows the Ferrari factory in 1989.

Although Ferrari produced the world's fastest car in 1984, in the shape of the 288GTO, it was soon edged off its pedestal by the four-wheel-drive Porsche 959. Ferrari, however, was not to be ousted permanently, as it proved by launching the even more fantastic F40 model in 1987.

The name told its own story, for it was effectively the 40th anniversary of the birth of the famous car maker. When it first appeared, however, it looked so stark, and was so obviously designed and developed with competitions in mind, that it was assumed very few would be made.

The pundits couldn't have been more wrong. Ferrari settled down to build not a handful, but hundreds of these phenomenal machines, selling them only to chosen customers, and those whom Ferrari thought deserved the privilege of owning such a machine. The F40's chassis was an up-dated and up-gunned version of that used for the 288GTO, but clothed in a new body style. The wheelbase and the suspension were much as before, as was the engine and rear-drive transmission layout. The engine, however, had been slightly enlarged, and had been tuned

Every detail of the F40 was functional, including air scoops for the brakes and for the air-conditioning equipment.

67

further still. Four hundred bhp for the 288GTO had been exceptional, but the 478bhp claimed for the F40's unit was quite out of the ordinary. This was equal to 161bhp/litre, a higher rating than that offered by any other road car anywhere in the world.

On top of that, for a great deal of money Ferrari was also prepared to supply a race-tuned engine offering an extra 200bhp.

Once again Pininfarina had been entrusted with the styling job and had produced a low nosed 2-seater coupé, with air scoops in each flank, and a massive free-standing rear spoiler. The bodywork itself was made out of carbon fibre, or Kevlar, depending on the strength required in any particular section, the interior was stripped out, with only the minimum of furnishing, and the ensemble simply cried out – 'racer'!

It was the ideal car to wrest the 'world's fastest car' title from Porsche, and no one doubted that the F40 would exceed 200mph (322kmh) and continue handling like a thoroughbred race car right up to those speeds.

Naturally the F40 also had searing acceleration, and the roadholding could be tuned to the conditions. In spite of the fact that it was by no means luxuriously equipped, the F40 was fitted with full air-conditioning. This, in any case, was essential, as the heat output from the 179CID/2.9-litre engine, which was mounted just behind the seats, was very high indeed.

It all depended on how you measured it, but the F40 was probably the most powerful car ever sold to the public in any numbers. In the late 1980s, by any standards, it was also the fastest car in the world.

RIGHT
The business-end of the vee-8 twin-turbo engined Ferrari F40, showing the exhaust system and the twin cooling scoops.

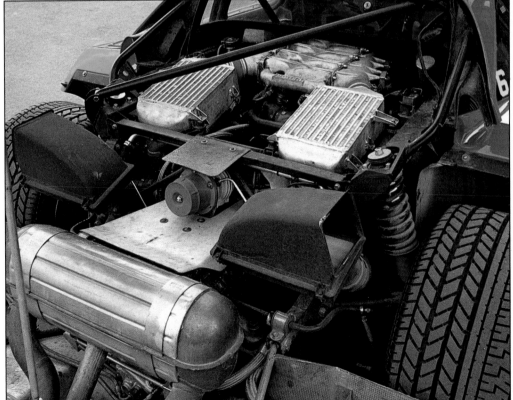

Ford Mustang Mach 1 and Boss

PRODUCTION SPAN
1968 – 1971

ENGINE
V8-cyl, 2 ohv

CAPACITY
302, 351, 390, 428 and 429CID
(4,945, 5,750, 6,388, 7,010
and 7,027cc)

MAXIMUM POWER
290–375bhp

CHASSIS SUSPENSION
Unit construction steel structure, coil
spring/wishbone ifs, leaf spring/beam
axle rear suspension

BODY STYLE
2-door, 4-seater coupé

TOP SPEED
335bhp 428CID Mach 1: 115mph
(185kmh)

0–60mph
5.7 sec

Ford's original Mustang was the most successful new model ever introduced by the Detroit concern. More than a million were sold in less than two years, the car actually establishing a new 'pony car' name for the enthusiasts to talk about.

Although the Mustang had a very conventional chassis/running gear layout, right from the start it was available with a huge variety of engines. In every model year from 1965 to 1973 there was a choice of straight-six, and V8 engines. As the years went by, and the Mustang became successful in motorsport, the V8 power options became more powerful.

Apart from the specialised Shelby models, the first truly rapid Mustang was the Boss 302 model of 1969, this being an 'homologation special' designed with SCCA Trans-Am

racing in mind. Although the 302CID V8 engine was placarded at 'only' 290bhp, it actually produced something closer to 400bhp! Added to this was the fitment of extra aerodynamic spoilers front and rear, stiffened up suspension, wider tyres and better brakes.

Later in the life of the Mustang, the 'Boss' also became available with the gargantuan (and heavy) 429CID engine, a car called 'devastating' by Mustang historians, probably the best all-round Mustang ever built.

Also new for 1969 was the Mach 1, a sleek, highly-decorated, fastback coupé aimed at the 'boy racer' brigade. Unlike the Boss, the original Mach 1 was more for show than for go, though its standard engine was a broad-shouldered 351CID V8 – an early example of the 'Cleveland' design.

The 1969 Mach 1 was also available with the mighty 335bhp 428CID 'Cobra Jet' engine, which made the car one of the fastest accelerating machines in the world.

Between 1969 and 1973 Mustangs got larger, even better equipped, and heavier, but because of the strangling effect of the new exhaust emission regulations, power ratings reached their peak in 1971, and fell rapidly after that time.

In the three climactic years of 1969, 1970 and 1971, however, the Boss and the Mach 1 models ruled the performance car roost in the USA, for only the Chevrolet Camaro Z28, and the Pontiac Firebird Trans-Am could compete with them in the 'pony-car' category.

This was the period in which the young of North America could 'lay rubber' at every traffic light, rumble and bellow their way around every suburban corner, and generally demonstrate how Ford could offer so much performance, for so little money. In a way, even Ford was slightly ashamed by such exuberance – and the Mustang would never be the same car again.

ABOVE LEFT
All the Mustangs were compact four-seaters – this being a 1969 model, complete with automatic transmission and Mustang decals on the door trims, which were in simulated wood.

ABOVE
The fastest Mustangs had large-capacity vee-8 engines to give them truly remarkable acceleration. This engine is one of the famous 351CID/5.7-litre 'Cleveland' units, the type which powered the original Mach 1 model.

LEFT
The last of the big, broad-shouldered Mustangs was built in 1973 and, as ever, it was available in hardtop or convertible form. In nine years, from 1964, it had become larger and heavier, but was still a very powerful car. Those bonnet scoops directed fresh air into a well-filled engine bay.

BELOW
1971 'Boss' Mustang; six body styles were available at the beginning of the decade, the hardtop coupe being the most popular.

Hispano-Suiza V12

PRODUCTION SPAN
1931 – 1938

ENGINE
V12-cyl, ohv

CAPACITY
575CID (9424cc) or 690CID (11310cc)

MAXIMUM POWER
190–220bhp or 250bhp

CHASSIS SUSPENSION
Separate steel chassis, leaf spring/beam axle front suspension, leaf spring/beam axle rear suspension

BODY STYLE
Various, saloon, limousine and open tourer

TOP SPEED
220bhp model: 100mph (161 kmh)

0–60mph
220bhp model: 12.0 sec

Having built some of the world's finest cars between 1904 and 1930, Hispano-Suiza faced up to the Depression with defiance. It was typical of designer Marc Birkigt. Instead of trying to design downmarket (a policy which killed off several other concerns at this time), Hispano-Suiza went upmarket with its most prestigious car – a vast chassis with a choice of four different wheelbase lengths, and a magnificent new V12 engine.

Although the marque name, when translated, means 'Spanish-Swiss', Hispano-Suiza actually built cars in Spain and in France. It was decided to produce the new car and its Type 68 engine in the French factory.

Although the chassis itself was strictly conventional by late 1920s/early 1930s standards – it had a beam axle at front and rear, suspended on leaf springs – it was distinguished by the use of a gearbox-driven brake servo (the same type, incidentally, built under licence by Rolls Royce for so many years).

By European standards, the new V12 engine was a monster, outranked only by the gargantuan Bugatti Royale

A B O V E
This impressive Van Vooren bodied example of the vee-12 Hispano Suiza was built in 1933. It was one of the most expensive, and certainly the fastest, cars in the world at the time.

unit (which was not really a private car design at all). Unlike previous Hispano-Suiza units, which had overhead camshaft valve gear, the V12 made do with a conventional pushrod/overhead valve layout.

The engine itself had integral blocks and heads of light alloy, screwed in nitralloy cylinder lines, and tubular connecting rods. For the first four years this engine was a 9.4-litre unit, but from 1935 it was given a longer stroke, and became a 11.3-litre unit, with no less than 250bhp.

By any motoring standards of the day this made the Hispano-Suiza the most powerful car in the world. Even though complete cars weighed up to 5000lb, (2268kg), all

Some of the most exciting vee-12 engined Hispano Suizas of all had convertible body styles. This British registered car was built in 1934 – it cost its lucky owner considerably more than the fastest Rolls-Royce of the day.

had top speeds of at least 100mph (16kmh), with acceleration which was quite startling. Road test reports were spattered with words like 'magnificent', 'phenomenal' and 'astonishing'.

Although very few examples of the V12, in fact, were built, and it was hardly the sort of car which could prosper in 1930s Europe, it was an impressive and well-engineered standard-setter for the world's car makers. For swishing up and down the fast roads of France, between Paris and the Riviera resorts, it was an ideal magic carpet.

Hispano-Suiza, nevertheless, found it more profitable to build aero engines than cars, and dropped the V12 in 1938.

Jaguar XK120

PRODUCTION SPAN
1948 – 1954

ENGINE
6-cyl, 2 ohc

CAPACITY
210CID (3442cc)

MAXIMUM POWER
160 or 180bhp

CHASSIS SUSPENSION
Separate steel chassis frame, torsion bar/wishbone ifs, leaf spring/beam axle rear suspension

BODY STYLE
2-door, 2-seater roadster, coupé or convertible

TOP SPEED
160bhp: 120mph (193kmh)

0–60mph
160bhp: 9.9 sec

BOTTOM
Jaguar's famous XK engine was the first twin-overhead camshaft design to be put into series production. In 1948, when launched, it produced 160bhp, and the XK120 sports car which used it could exceed 120mph.

BELOW
A British Union Flag, and proud of it, fitted to this particular Jaguar, though not a standard fitting.

During the Second World War, Jaguar's founder, William Lyons, laid plans for a range of new cars. The centrepiece of this strategy was a new family of 4- and 6-cylinder engines, though at first there was no thought of building a sports car.

Then, in 1948, with the chassis nearly ready, and the engine due for preview, it was decided to produce a sports car after all. In a matter of weeks a chassis was shortened, a body style conceived, and the result was the XK120.

The new 2-seater was originally meant to be a limited production machine, but was eventually made in much larger quantities. In 13 years the famous XK series of cars went through three different editions – XK120, XK140 and XK150 – and was the sports car which established Jaguar's reputation in the USA.

The new engine, also coded XK, was intended not only to be powerful but to look powerful too. The cylinder block was cast iron, but the cylinder head was light alloy, and the twin overhead camshafts were covered by polished alloy castings. The 4-cylinder version of this engine never went into production, but the straight 'six' had a life of more than 40 years, eventually being built in sizes from 2.4 to 4.2 litres.

For the original XK120, the engine was a beautifully detailed 3.4-litre unit, producing 160bhp (SAE), which was a lot more than any previous Jaguar engine had ever developed. It was not long before sports car enthusiasts discovered that the new unit was not just silkily silent but extremely tuneable. First with the C-type, and then even more gloriously with the D-type, Jaguar showed that the engine could power world class endurance race winning machinery.

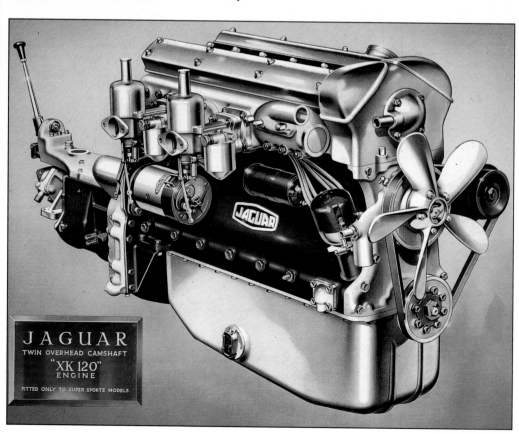

JAGUAR
TWIN OVERHEAD CAMSHAFT
"XK 120" ENGINE
FITTED ONLY TO SUPER SPORTS MODELS

ABOVE
The XK120's famous engine, the very first twin-cam unit to go into series production. In much-developed form it remained in production until the end of the 1980s.

ABOVE
The XK120 fixed-head coupe was the second type to be put on sale. This particular example made its name by completing seven days and seven nights at the French Montlhery circuit at an average speed of 100mph.

LEFT
The XK120's beautifully detailed nose included a grille with very slim bars (though some cars overheated in Californian heatwaves), extra-strong headlamps, and slim but functional bumpers, all included in an incredibly low price.

Details of the original XK120 catalogue show that the new Jaguar, though simply engineered, was carefully detailed. This was not only a sleek two-seater, but a very functional and well-equipped sports car.

LEFT
The XK120 was Jaguar's first postwar sports car, which was not only fitted with the sensational new twin-cam engine, but with a very well equipped facia and instrument package.

The XK120 itself had a solid and conventional chassis frame, but used independent front suspension by torsion bars and wishbones, a layout apparently influenced by Citroen's invention of the 1930s. Drum brakes were still standard (disc brakes were not yet available for motor cars). The new car had sensuously curved styling and leather-trimmed seats, and was sold at astonishingly low prices.

In the beginning there was only one body type, the 2-seater open roadster, which featured detachable side curtains and a simple soft top. But by the early 1950s the fixed-head coupé and the lushly trimmed drop head coupé had also been added.

Jaguar also made the engine available in 180bhp 'special equipment' form, which was popular with those wanting to use their XK120s in motor sport. Perhaps the XK120 was not as fast as the V12 Ferraris, or the Mercedes-Benz 300SL sports cars, but it was dramatically cheaper, made in larger numbers, and appealed to many more people.

Jaguar E-Type (6-cylinder)

PRODUCTION SPAN
1961–1971

ENGINE
6-cyl, 2 ohc

CAPACITY
231CID (3781cc) and 258CID (4235cc)

MAXIMUM POWER
265bhp

CHASSIS SUSPENSION
Multi-tube chassis frame bolted to steel centre monocoque, torsion bar/wishbone ifs, coil spring/locating arm irs

BODY STYLE
2-door, 2-seater or 2+2 seater roadster or coupé

TOP SPEED
150mph (241kmh)

0–60mph
7.0 sec

During the 1950s, Jaguar built two very successful racing sports cars – the C-Type and D-type models. In long distance events such as the French Le Mans 24 Hour, and the USA Sebring 12 Hour events, the cars proved to be not only very fast but very durable.

To replace the D-type in the late 1950s, Jaguar began designing the E-type, but then withdrew from motor racing. In a very brave decision, the company decided to 'productionize' the new project. After a lot of re-design and re-development a sensational new sports car, the E-type (or XK-E, as it was called in the USA) was revealed in 1961.

The E-type was a direct replacement for the elegant old XK150, but was very different from that car. It used an updated version of the famous twin-cam XK engine, and the same 4-speed gearbox, but the structure, the suspension, and especially the styling were all new.

The style was effectively a longer, sleeker, smoothed-out version of the racing D-Type, though naturally equipped with a full-sized windscreen and a choice of open roadster or fastback coupé styles. The nose was long and curvaceous, the headlamps were hidden behind sloping glass covers, and the bumpers were carefully moulded around the contours. The shape had been established mathematically by one of Jaguar's specialists and was a great advance on that of its predecessor.

The structure had also developed from that of the D-Type, for there was a multi-tube front frame bolted to a steel monocoque centre section. On this car too, there was independent suspension at front and rear, with 4-wheel disc brakes.

BELOW
An unmistakable nose, that of the original 6-cylinder Jaguar E-Type, complete with glass covers over its headlamp, and with neat decoration across its oval radiator air intake.

LEFT
By the early 1970s the E-Type had progressed to become Series II, with an enlarged front air intake, exposed headlamps, larger turn indicators, and many improvements under the skin.

RIGHT
Compared with the original cars, Series II E-Types had the '4.2' litre badge on the bootlid, different taillamp clusters, and a revised rear panel shape.

ABOVE
The E-Type was such a compact supercar that the engine almost filled the available space.

The engine was a highly-developed version of the XK engine first used in the XK120 of 1948, this time of 3.8-litres, with three SU carburettors and no less than 265bhp (SAE). Three years after launch, the engine was enlarged to 4.2-litres, though the maximum power rating did not change; at the same time a new all-synchromesh gearbox was also fitted. Two years later, for the longer-wheelbase 2+2 type, automatic transmission also became available.

Although this peak power figure was less than that claimed for certain Ferraris, in conjunction with the body's wind-cheating shape it guaranteed a top speed of 145–150mph (233–241kmh), depending on conditions, with acceleration to match, all at a price which brought it within range of thousands of customers every year.

The E-Type was not perfect, for its sleek style meant that the cabin was cramped, the low nose meant that the engine could sometimes overheat, and the low price meant that quality and reliability compromises had to be made. Nevertheless, it became one of the greatest car virility symbols ever known, and was on sale for ten years.

ABOVE
If you bought an E-Type, it was advisable not to be too tall, as the driving position and cockpit area was quite small.

Jaguar E-Type 12-cylinder)

PRODUCTION SPAN
1971–1975

ENGINE
V12-cyl, ohc

CAPACITY
326CID (5343cc)

MAXIMUM POWER
272bhp

CHASSIS SUSPENSION
Multi-tube chassis frame bolted to steel centre monocoque, torsion bar/ wishbone ifs, coil spring/locating arm irs

BODY STYLE
2-door, 2-seater roadster or 2+2 seater coupé

TOP SPEED
146mph (239kmh)

0–60mph
6.4 sec

RIGHT
The classic vee-12 engined E-Type Roadster, as built by Jaguar from 1971 to 1975, shows off its new grille, flared wheel arches, and the steel disc wheels which were also available on this model. This was the open version, which was much more popular than the coupé type.

BELOW
The Series III E-Type was based on the original design, but had the vee-12 engine under the bonnet, with wider wheels and tyres, flared wheelarches, and a grille in the nose aperture. Open and fixed-head versions were available. Later US-market models (like these cars) needed extra rubber bumpers to meet regulations.

By 1971 the Jaguar E-Type had been on sale for a decade, the old XK engine had gradually become strangled by exhaust emission clean-up equipment, and it was all due for change. Rather than introduce a completely new car, Jaguar re-worked the existing design, with a longer wheelbase for the roadster, better suspension, and a brand-new and exciting V12 engine.

Although it was a classic case of 'new wine in an old bottle', the re-design worked remarkably well. The problem was that it was such an outstanding new design that the pundits started talking about an engine looking for a new chassis too! They only had to wait another year or so, for Jaguar then launched the XJ12 saloon car, which was just as refined as expected.

The revised E-Type was known as Series III, and although early adverts suggested that V12 6-cylinder engines would be available, the 6-cylinder types were never sold.

The E-Type looked more meaty, but less sleek, than before. All cars were now to be built on the longer wheelbase originally chosen for 2+2 models (which meant that the roadster was nine inches longer than before); wider wheels and tyres meant that the wheelarches had to be flared, while the front air intake was much larger than before.

BELOW
As the years progressed, not only did E-Type headlamps come out into the open, but they were also edged forward to improve their performance.

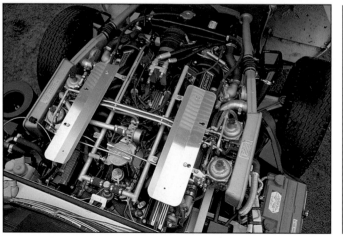

ABOVE
The Series III E-Type coupé was the final derivative of the 2+2 coupé which had gone on sale in 1966, complete with an 8ft. 9in. wheelbase and two tiny 'occasional rear seats.

LEFT
Jaguar's vee-12 engine was a very tight fit under the bonnet of the E-Type, with its carburation arranged to make the engine wide, rather than tall. There were four constant-vacuum type carburettors in this installation.

A B O V E
Simple, informative, badging on the Series III E-Type. Stand well clear, please . . .

The reason for all this was the adoption of a new light-alloy V12 engine, one originally intended for use in the company's saloons, but then hastily adapted for use in the E-Type sports car. It was a 326CID/3.5-litre masterpiece, with single overhead camshaft valve gear, and with four carburettors – two mounted outboard of each cylinder head, but with complex cross-over inlet passages.

It was Europe's first series-production V12 engine (those fitted to Ferraris and Lamborghinis were hand-built, by comparison), and had been developed with total refinement, flexibility and silence in mind. For that reason, it was only a little more powerful than the best of the 6-cylinder XKs, though it developed considerably more mid-range torque. The whole car was heavier than before, and rather less fuel-efficient (15mpg instead of 18mpg).

Even so, the Series III E-Type still offered phenomenal performance and value for money, enough at any rate to keep the model alive until the mid-1970s. Not only did it restore the E-Type's top speed (in unrestricted European form) to nearly 150mph (241kmh), but it had colossal acceleration (0–100mph in about 15 seconds), all allied to a fuss- and noise-free V12 engine.

The E-Type was phased out in the winter of 1974–1975, after 15,287 cars had been produced, but the V12 engine went on to greater things. It was still an important part of Jaguar's line-up as the 1990s opened.

T O P
This was the crowded fascia/instrument display of the Series III E-Type, complete with automatic transmission in this case, and the optional radio fitting. Since the car's top speed was nearly 150mph, a speedometer with all those markings was certainly justified.

A B O V E
The series III was available with wire-spoke wheels, or with steel disc wheels like these.

Lamborghini Miura

PRODUCTION SPAN
1966–1973

ENGINE
V12-cyl, 2 ohc

CAPACITY
240CID (3929cc)

MAXIMUM POWER
350, 370 and 385bhp

CHASSIS SUSPENSION
Steel platform-type chassis structure, coil spring/wishbone ifs, coil spring/wishbone irs

BODY STYLE
2-door, 2-seater coupé

TOP SPEED
370bhp: 172mph (277kmh)

0–60mph
6.7 sec

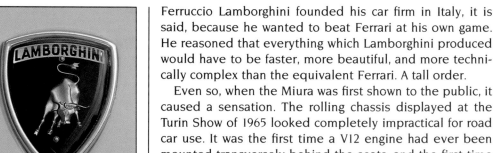

ABOVE
Lamborghini's famous mascot, the fighting bull.

RIGHT
The Miura, with its well-filled front end, in the foreground, with the later Jalpa model in the background.

BELOW
The Miura was the world's first transverse vee-12-engined car, and had quite stupendous performance.

Ferruccio Lamborghini founded his car firm in Italy, it is said, because he wanted to beat Ferrari at his own game. He reasoned that everything which Lamborghini produced would have to be faster, more beautiful, and more technically complex than the equivalent Ferrari. A tall order.

Even so, when the Miura was first shown to the public, it caused a sensation. The rolling chassis displayed at the Turin Show of 1965 looked completely impractical for road car use. It was the first time a V12 engine had ever been mounted transversely behind the seats, and the first time such a layout had been proposed for general sale.

The prototype, complete with dramatically-styled 2-door coupé shell (by Bertone, but penned by Marcello Gandini) was ready in a matter of months, and deliveries began before the end of 1966. The new car was a resounding success, and was ousted only by an even more amazing super-car, the Countach. 763 cars were built in less than seven years.

The centrepiece of the design, in every way, was the quad-cam V12 engine, a 240CID/4-litre version of that originally shown in 1963. It had a light alloy cylinder block and cylinder heads, topped by a forest of dual-choke Weber carburettors, and was a beautifully made, flexible, powerful and utterly reliable piece of machinery.

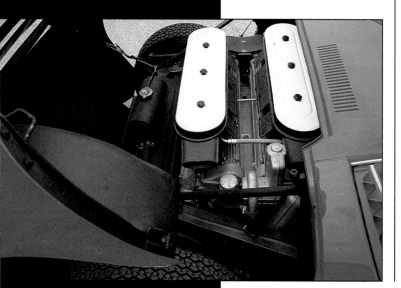

The Miura was too heavy for motor racing (and, in any case, the boss himself forbade it), but it had a great race-standard chassis. The style shouted 'race car' to every on-looker, while under the skin there was a wide and squat layout, with wide tyres, all-independent suspension, vast brakes and inch-accurate rack-and-pinion steering.

The shape, too, was efficient. Every Miura could reach 170mph (273kmh) – though the car became 'light', and was ready to take off if such speeds were reached – with the flashing acceleration and all the right sort of howling noises that one might expect. It was true that the driving position was cramped, and ventilation was poor, but to own such a charismatic machine, it was said, there had to be compromises.

Over the years the Muira got quicker and better. The original P400 boasted 350bhp, but from 1970 this became the P400S with 370bhp, while the final P400SVs of 1971 and 1972 had 385bhp engines. Those, incidentally, were 'in-stalled' bhp figures, quoted without exaggeration, and explain why the Miura was so incredibly fast.

Was it the world's fastest car at the time? Some say yes, and some say no. The only obvious rival was Ferrari's front-engined Daytona. But then, at anything over 150mph (240kmh), when a driver is far too busy to worry about trifles, was anyone arguing?

TOP
Lamborghini's Miura was an astonishing car by any 1960s standards, not least for its lines, and for details like the lie-back headlamps. The engine was transversely mounted, behind the cabin.

ABOVE
No need for ostentation on the rear of the Miura S, just a badge, and two understated exhaust pipes to get the message across.

LEFT
The badge reads 'Bertone', the black scoop directs air into the engine bay, and the flared arches cover wide wheels and tyres. Everything had a function on the Miura.

Lamborghini Countach

PRODUCTION SPAN
1974–1989

ENGINE
V12-cyl, 2 ohc

CAPACITY
240CID (3929cc), 290CID (4754cc),
315CID (5167cc)

MAXIMUM POWER
375 and 455bhp

CHASSIS SUSPENSION
Multi-tube chassis structure, coil
spring/wishbone ifs, coil spring/
wishbone irs

BODY STYLE
2-door, 2-seater coupé

TOP SPEED
455bhp: 178mph (286kmh)

0–60mph
455bhp: 4.9 sec

The anatomy of a real supercar, a near-finished Lamborghini Countach at the S'Agata factory, ready to receive its fold forward-type doors, and a few final fittings, before beginning a 180mph career.

If such a car was possible, the original Lamborghini Countach was even more extraordinary than the Miura which it was to replace. It used the same type of four-cam V12 engine as the Miura, and was equally as fast, but had even more outlandish styling. Once again it was Marcello Gandini of Bertone who had devised the shape, intending it to sell to the same breed of wealthy drivers who would love the car for its looks as much as for its performance.

The various code names applied to Countach models – LP400, LP500S and so on – give a clue to the mechanical layout, for LP stands for 'Longitudinal Posteriore' (Italian for 'rear-mounted, in line'), and refers to the engine layout.

In this car the massive V12 engine was mounted in-line, rather than transversely, still behind the seats, but this time driving forward to a gearbox, then by a long quill shaft to the final drive between the rear wheels.

Whereas the Miura's style had been all voluptuous, swooping curves, the new car had more brutal, more angular lines. The door opening mechanism was unique, for on this car the hinges were horizontal, so that the doors opened vertically upwards and forwards, rather like the wings of a beetle.

It was not surprising that Lamborghini's workers reacted so strongly to this car. 'Countach', in Italian, can be described as a more polite expletive, as the equivalent of 'wow' or 'amazing' – which the car undoubtedly was.

In the late 1970s the Countach had only two rivals for supremacy – the Ferrari Boxer and the Maserati Bora – but since all could reach, and exceed, 170mph (273kmh), back-to-back shoot-outs were rarely attempted. All these cars had mid-engined/rear-drive layouts, handled like rather overweight race cars, and had stupendous acceleration.

BELOW
Extra wide Pirelli tyres on cast-alloy wheels, a rear spoiler to give added downforce, and brutally-stated Bertone lines, all spell out the potential performance of Lamborghini's Countach.

RIGHT
On every model of Countach, the doors opened forward and upward, beetle-fashion; this feature was never copied by any other production-car maker.

ABOVE
Every detail of the style of the Countach was carefully studied. This was the location of the side/indicator lamps, behind a fluted glass cover; the flip-up headlamps were further back along the wing panel.

LEFT
The Countach's vee-12 engine was longitudinally mounted, driving forward to its gearbox.

As the years progressed, the Lamborghini's extremely powerful quad-cam V12 engine had to be modified to keep abreast of exhaust emission regulations. To regain the power lost in such de-tuning and de-toxing, Lamborghini first enlarged the engine (to 4.7-litres and LP500S) in 1982, then in 1985 enlarged it again and equipped it with 4-valve cylinder heads. Thus the ultimate Countach, the 455bhp 5000 Quattrovalvole, was born, the car by which all other supercars had to measure themselves for a while.

Every Countach was an outstanding performer, but some looked more outlandish than others, for a variety of spoilers, rear wings and add-on equipment became available.

The Countach was finally ousted by the Diablo at the end of the 1980s, having enjoyed a 15-year career. At the end, as in the beginning, it was one of the very few truly super-fast cars on sale throughout the world.

ABOVE
Countach in production at S'Agata in Italy, managing to look even more menacing in black than in red.

RIGHT
A beautiful name for a beautiful car.

Marmon Sixteen

PRODUCTION SPAN
1931–1933

ENGINE
V16-cyl, ohv

CAPACITY
491CID (8049cc)

MAXIMUM POWER
200bhp

CHASSIS SUSPENSION
Separate steel chassis, leaf spring/beam axle front suspension, leaf spring/beam axle rear suspension

BODY STYLE
Various – saloon, coupé, convertible

TOP SPEED
100mph (160kmh)

0–60mph
Not recorded

Howard Marmon's car making concern was founded in 1902, and often built fast and technically advanced cars. Marmon, however, was one of the unluckiest of all firms. It developed one of America's most complex and expensive new cars just when the nation descended into the Depression – and when Cadillac was embarking on the same design path.

Work began on a 16-cylinder-engined Marmon in 1926, and it was launched for 1931. The Sixteen model, magnificent though it was, was almost exactly the sort of car guaranteed to fail in the time of economic decline which followed the Wall Street crash.

All the Sixteens rode on a massive 145in (368cm) wheelbase chassis, and with a range of different body styles prices started at $5,220. This, please note, compared with the $430 asked for a mass-produced Model A Ford. Obviously it was a car destined to sell in very small numbers, to the very wealthy – and by 1931 there were few such individuals left in North America.

The Sixteen's engine was a masterpiece. It had 16 cylinders, placed in 45-degree vee-formation, with the main castings almost entirely built from light alloy; the assembly weighed 930lb (422kg). There was overhead valve gear, but only a single downdraught carburettor. Nevertheless, Marmon claimed 200bhp (SAE) for this 491CID monster – a rating which put it well in front of the V16 Cadillac (an obvious competitor), and at least on a par with the contemporary Hispano Suiza V12 of the day. The only other supercar of the day to beat the Marmon's output was the 8-litre Bentley, and that was about to go out of production.

By the standards of 1931, the Marmon was advanced and impressive, for its bodies were styled by the Teagues, father and son, the gearbox included the new-fangled synchromesh (licenced from General Motors), and Marmon guaranteed that the top speed was up around the 100mph mark (160kmh). It was, of course, a very thirsty beast (8mpg if you were thoughtful, worse than this if you were in a hurry . . .).

Unhappily, Marmon folded just as the Depression began to lift, for sales fell steadily throughout the early 1930s. The Sixteen, like other 'white elephants' such as the Duesenberg SJ, retreated into mythology, and into unimaginable values today as a collectors' piece.

The vee-16 engined Marmon was one of North America's most exclusive cars in the early 1930s. The engine was an 8-litre/491 CID unit, with overhead valve gear.

Maserati Ghibli

PRODUCTION SPAN
1966–1973

ENGINE
V8-cyl, 2 ohc

CAPACITY
287CID (4709cc) or 301CID (4930cc)

MAXIMUM POWER
330 or 335bhp

CHASSIS SUSPENSION
Tubular steel/fabricated chassis frame, coil spring/wishbone ifs, leaf spring/ beam axle rear suspension

BODY STYLE
2-door, 2+2 seater coupé or convertible

TOP SPEED
4.7-litre: 154mph (248kmh)

0–60mph
4.7-litre: 7.5 sec

RIGHT
This particular Ghibli was a rare bird, for it had right-hand steering. The 'office' was functional, but comprehensive.

ABOVE
The Ghibli's tail gave little away.

BELOW
The Ghibli had smooth, beautiful, lines, when viewed from any angle. Ghia had every reason to be proud of it.

During the 1960s and 1970s Maserati built a series of fine front-engined cars, all with V8 engines of a variety of sizes. In every case the bodies, or the semi-monoque structures, were provided by coachbuilding specialists, while Maserati concentrated on building the running gear.

All were fast, but some were faster than others. All looked good, but just a few looked great. It was the combination of high performance, sensationally sleek styling and great supercar character which made the Ghibli a magnificent car.

The 'base' car for the Ghibli was the original Quattroporte saloon, which had been launched in 1963, but although this had Maserati's fine quad-cam V8 engine, this was a bulky and rather ponderous 4-door saloon car.

A shorter version of the chassis, with beam axle rear suspension instead of the original De Dion, was then developed. Two different bodies were then evolved – the rather mundane 4-seater Mexico coupé (bodied by Vignale), and the beautiful two-seater Ghibli style, by Ghia. In later years enthusiasts learned that it had actually been designed by Giorgetto Giugiaro, who later went on to found Ital design.

Over the years Ghibli was to be built as a closed, fast-back coupé, or as a convertible. Although coupés were the most numerous, the fashion for 'collectors' cars' means that the convertible is now thought to be more desirable. As with the 5000GT, already described, the chassis of the Ghibli was relatively simple and conventional, though by this time a 4-disc brake installation had been chosen, and automatic transmission was available as optional equipment.

Compared with the 5000GT's engine, the V8 had been refined even more, put into what passed for series production at Maserati, and was fitted with four dual-choke Weber carburettors. It was flexible and without temperament, and

made lots of exciting little noises to convince the owner of the potential which was locked inside.

Until Ferrari produced the Daytona, two years after the launch of the Ghibli, there was no doubt that it was one of the most beautiful front-engined cars in the world. The nose was long and low, with a shallow full-width grille and pop-headlamps mounted immediately behind that grille. Cooling outlets along the flanks emphasized the length and the sweeping lines, while at the back the tail was sharply cut off.

The Ghibli was as fast as it looked. Maserati had not provided over-high gearing, so that it had an astonishingly high top speed. Many owners found that they could rush up to 140mph (225kmh) at every opportunity, and cruise at close to that pace.

No wonder the Ghibli was so popular – and that 1274 cars were sold before the model was withdrawn in 1973.

ABOVE
Ground-level view of the Ghibli shows the carefully detailed nose and front quarter, with integrated bumpers, and cooling grilles in the front wings.

LEFT
A rack of switches, and cooling vents dominated the centre console.

RIGHT
The four-cam vee-8 engine (330bhp or 335bhp, to choice) filled the Ghibli's engine bay.

Maserati Bora

PRODUCTION SPAN
1971–1978

ENGINE
V8-cyl, 2 ohc

CAPACITY
287CID (4709cc), or 301CID (4930cc)

MAXIMUM POWER
310 or 330bhp

CHASSIS SUSPENSION
Unit construction steel structure, coil
spring/wishbone ifs, coil spring/
wishbone irs

BODY STYLE
2-door, 2-seater coupé

TOP SPEED
4.7-litre: 162mph (257kmh)

0–60mph
4.7-litre: 6.5 sec

ABOVE
**No spare space in the engine bay of
the Bora.**

BELOW
**Not classically beautiful, but certainly
squat and impressive, the Bora was a
high-performance mid-engined
masterpiece. Top speed? More than
160mph.**

Once Lamborghini had produced the mid-engined Miura, other Italian manufacturers of supercars had to follow suit. Maserati took its time, thought out a design carefully, and did not launch the mid-engined Bora until 1971.

By this time Maserati had been acquired by Citroen of France, who provided a great deal of encouragement and investment capital. It was inevitable, therefore, that some Citroen details should appear in the new car, including some typically complex hydraulic details.

Although the Bora was powered by Maserati's familiar V8 engine – originally in 4.7-litre form, as used in cars like the Ghibli – the rest of the design was new. In particular, the 5-speed gearbox was by ZF of West Germany (the same type as used in cars like the Ford GT40), while the structure was a pressed and fabricated steel monocoque. Naturally there was four-wheel independent suspension, and a fully trimmed and furnished interior.

The styling was by Giugiaro, at his new Ital Design complex, and Maserati decided to use a derivative of the layout, with a V6 engine of smaller capacity, for the Merak, which was much less powerful and a lot slower than the Bora.

Even though it was meant to be a full-blooded contender for the unofficial 'fastest supercar' competition, and looked like a street-going version of a race car, the Bora was a very practical mid-engined machine, with a great deal of stowage space, electric window lifts, and a comfortable 2-seater cockpit. There was even space for (heat-proof) bags to be placed on a shelf above the engine bay.

The original Bora had 310bhp, and soon proved that it could exceed 160mph (257kmh), but with an eye to selling cars in the USA, Maserati set about 'de-toxing' the V8. At the same time, to make sure that no unnecessary power was lost, the engine was enlarged to 4.9-litres. This 330bhp engine derivative became available from 1976.

Independent road tests proved the car's very high top speeds and pinpointed the extraordinary flexibility of the engine. If necessary, top (fifth) gear could be engaged at less than 20mhp (32kmh), and the car would then pull strongly and evenly all the way up the scale. It took no longer to accelerate from 20–40mph (32–64kmh) in fifth gear than it did from 100–120mhp (160–192kmh).

ABOVE
Not only was the Bora a very fast car, but it was extremely practical. Front and rear panelling opened to give easy access for service, while the cockpit was roomy enough for two people.

BELOW
This British registration plate – WOW – says it all, for the Bora was a real man's car, with enormous performance and a character to suit.

Maserati Khamsin

PRODUCTION SPAN
1973–1982

ENGINE
V8-cyl, 2 ohc

CAPACITY
301CID (4930cc)

MAXIMUM POWER
320bhp

CHASSIS SUSPENSION
Unit construction steel structure, coil spring/wishbone ifs, coil spring/wishbone irs

BODY STYLE
2-door, 2+2-seater coupé

TOP SPEED
160mph (257kmh)

0–60mph
8.1 sec

Not only was the Khamsin one of the prettiest front-engined Maseratis of all, but it sold well, and remained in production for nearly ten years. Like all such Maseratis, it was V8 powered, but it was the first of their cars to have Bertone styling.

Maserati was controlled financially, and influenced in technical terms, by Citroen from the late 1960s and 1975. The Khamsin was an important model in many ways, for Bertone produced a simply stunning and sharp-edged style for the car, the only new front-engined car designed and put into production in that period.

The Khamsin was delicately shaped by Bertone, in a remarkable front-engined style which made cars like the Ferrari Daytona look immediately out of date, and which seemed to guarantee fabulous performance. Unlike some other Italian supercars, this one had a unit-construction body/chassis structure.

Bertone of Turin styled the car, and was responsible for building the complex unit-construction body/chassis units, painting, trimming and furnishing the assemblies, before delivering them to Modena for completion.

The Khamsin was longer, lower, wider and more aggressively beautiful than the Ghibli of the 1960s, still with the characteristic wide nose, and the hidden headlamps above it. Unlike the Ghibli, however, it was built only as a closed car. In more mundane circumstances it would have been dubbed a hatchback, because there was a large full-width glass tailgate, and although there were two awkwardly shaped and upright '+2' seats it was better to consider the car as a generously-proportioned 2-seater coupé, with a lot of stowage space. Full air-conditioning was standard for a car which was definitely conceived with sales to hot climates in mind.

The venerable V8 engine, first seen in the mid-1950s, was still a very effective unit, and for the Khamsin it was used in 301CID/4.93-litre form. Surprisingly (for many other makers were going over to fuel injection) the engine still used four dual-choke Weber carburettors, well hidden under a massive air filter.

The Khamsin was the first front-engined Maserati to have four-wheel independent suspension. Naturally it had a

LEFT
The rear of the Khamsin obviously preferred to remain anonymous, but no-one could deny its beauty, or its high-performance promise.

RIGHT
The air intake ducting almost hides the engine, but there *is* a large, efficient, and extremely powerful four-cam vee-8 in there too!

ABOVE
The famous Maserati Trident badge.

LEFT
Khamsin owners, it seems, did not expect to have any bumper protection for their Bertone-styled body panels.

LEFT
Emphasizing that the Khamsin was a gentleman's supercar – a radio fitment, and automatic transmission!

choice of manual or automatic transmission, there were disc brakes for all four wheels, while Citroen SM-style power-assisted steering and brakes also betrayed some of its heritage.

Like other Maseratis of the period, with this marvellously flexible engine, the Khamsin seemed to have seven league boots when required, but was equally at home in heavy town traffic. It was very comfortable to drive fast (it was a much more practical car, if the truth be told, than the mid-engined Bora), and was a very well-developed car in most respects.

It was the last of the 'traditional' Maseratis to survive, at Modena, after the Argentinian tycoon Alejandro De Tomaso took control in the mid-1970s.

LEFT
Although this Khamsin followed in the tradition of all Italian supercars, it betrayed one modern trend – automatic transmission was an option.

BELOW
Very fast, yet eminently practical, the Maserati Khamsin was an elegant example of the 'glassback' theme.

Mercedes-Benz 'Grosser' 770

PRODUCTION SPAN
1930–1940

ENGINE
8-cyl, ohv

CAPACITY
467CID (7655cc)

MAXIMUM POWER
150–155bhp (unsupercharged) or 200–230bhp (supercharged)

CHASSIS SUSPENSION
Separate steel chassis. Before 1938: leaf spring/beam axle front suspension, leaf spring/beam axle rear suspension. From 1938: coil spring/wishbone ifs, coil spring/De Dion rear suspension

BODY STYLE
Various, saloon, limousine and convertible

TOP SPEED
100mph (160kmh)

0–60mph
Not recorded

Throughout the 1930s, Mercedes-Benz had an extremely large, heavy and costly flagship – the Type 770 – on offer. Production of this monstrous machine was very limited. Only 117 of the original type and 88 of the 1937–1940 variety were ever produced.

In the first place these were cars intended for state and ceremonial use, though a few were also sold to very wealthy businessmen. By the late 1930s, however, the 'Grosser' (as it had become known) had taken its place as transport for 'top people' in the Nazi party. Small wonder that most of the surviving examples are now supposed to be 'ex-Hitler' or 'ex-Goering'!

The original car had a vintage-style chassis layout, with beam axles at front and rear, whereas the 1937–1940 model had a technically advanced chassis built up from oval and circular section tubes, along with independent front and De Dion rear suspension.

Common to both types, however, was the big and heavy straight 8-cylinder engine, an overhead-valve unit which had a cast iron cylinder block bolted to a light alloy crankcase. It was specially designed, and dedicated, to these large cars, so Mercedes-Benz never installed more than rudimentary tooling.

As with other large capacity Mercedes-Benz models of the period, this engine was fitted with an optional supercharger arrangement. In normal use, at part throttle, the engine operated as a normally aspirated unit; when full throttle was applied, this brought a Roots-type supercharger into play, and the engine was much more powerful. It also became much noisier. If not in normally aspirated, but certainly in supercharged use, this was one of the world's most powerful engines.

Every example of the 'Grosser' (the word means 'large' or to be strictly accurate 'larger') was bulky and heavy, so the large engine was needed to provide an acceptable performance. Early examples weighed about 6000lb (2721kg), but at the end of the 1930s, when the Nazi leaders thought that armour plating was needed, individual cars weighed up to 8000lb (3629kg) and more.

As the late-model cars had a wheelbase of 155in (394cm), could be more than 20ft (60m) long, and were not equipped with power assisted steering, it was no wonder that there was no great rush to volunteer for chauffeur duty on these machines. The fitment of a 5-speed gearbox helped, but one needed to be rich to own a 'Grosser', as fuel economy could often drop to around 5mpg.

The 'Grosser' went out of production when the Second World War began, and was not revived.

Mercedes-Benz 300SL

PRODUCTION SPAN
1954–1963

ENGINE
6-cyl, ohc

CAPACITY
183CID (2996cc)

MAXIMUM POWER
240–250bhp

CHASSIS SUSPENSION
Separate steel-tube 'space-frame' chassis, coil spring/wishbone ifs, coil spring/swing axle irs

BODY STYLE
2-door, 2-seater coupé or (from 1957) roadster

TOP SPEED
129mph (207kmh) (depending on gearing)

0–60mph
8.8 sec

ABOVE
This was why the original 300SL coupé was called a 'gullwing' – the doors opened upwards, and took on the elegant profile of a gull's wing.

BELOW
Like the Grand Prix cars which Mercedes-Benz was making at the same time, the 300SL's steering wheel could be hinged away to provide better access to the driving seat.

Like Jaguar's E-type, the Mercedes-Benz 300SL was originally conceived as a racing car. The works team used it extensively, and successfully, in the 1952 season, then turned it over for conversion into a road car.

In this process the bodywork was converted from light-alloy to steel panelling, while the engine was made more powerful, with direct fuel injection. In two forms, first as the legendary 'gull-wing' coupé, and later as a more practical

RIGHT
Getting at the 300SL's engine bays was easy enough, but it needed practice to get into the seats.

ABOVE
All kitted-out to go on its next classic motorsporting event, this 300SL shows off the lines which made it so attractive when launched in 1954.

BOTTOM RIGHT
The 300SL's 'gull-wing' doors looked impressive, but were not popular with customers.

roadster, the 300SL had a successful nine year career, with 3250 produced.

The 300SL had a powerful and advanced engine, and was the first car in the world ever to be built around what became known as a 'space frame chassis'. This was a three-dimensional lattice assembly of tiny-diameter tubes connecting all the major stress points, positioned so that each tube was under tension or compression, providing lightness and rigidity.

BELOW
Every line and detail of the 300SL 'gullwing' had a function. The doors could not be made any deeper because of the position of the frame tubes, the grilles were fitted to extract hot air from the engine bay, and the wheel arch strakes helped to redirect water thrown up from the road.

For the frame to be stiff enough, it also had to have depth at mid-wheelbase point, which explains why the door sills were very high. On the original coupé the doors were hinged in the roof, and opened upwards (this gives rise to the nickname 'Gullwing'), but on the redesigned roadster of 1957 the layout was changed, with the doors front-hinged in the conventional manner.

The engine, transmission and much of the suspension were all modified versions of those already used in the 300 model, which was currently Mercedes-Benz's flagship model. However for the 300SL the 3-litre engine was installed partly on its side, and made much more powerful. In the 300S the engine produced 165bhp (SAE), but for the 300SL it was super-tuned to produce no less than 240bhp (SAE).

The 300SL went on sale in 1954, with a choice of rear axle ratios. Mercedes-Benz claimed 165mph (265kmh) with the highest possible gearing, but 130mph (209kmh) was a more normal maximum with the 'standard' gearing. At the time the 300SL was probably the fastest accelerating road car in the world (until, that is, Ferrari started selling Super-america models!).

The original chassis layout, however, was not up to the standards of performance, for its high-pivot swing axle rear suspension made it hard to handle at high speeds. The roadster of 1957 had a more practical cockpit layout, and featured low-pivot rear suspension, which made the car easier to handle.

For skilled drivers the 300SL was a fast and exhilarating car to drive, and built itself a splendid reputation in production car racing and in rallying. The space-free chassis was expensive to maintain and to repair, but the car had such a glamorous image that no one seemed to mind.

Mercedes-Benz 500SL and 560SL

PRODUCTION SPAN
1980–1982

ENGINE
V8-cyl, ohc

CAPACITY
304CID (4973cc), 339CID (5547cc)

MAXIMUM POWER
245 and 230bhp

CHASSIS SUSPENSION
Unit construction steel structure, coil spring/wishbone ifs, coil spring/semi-trailing arm irs

BODY STYLE
2-door, 2-seater roadster or coupé

TOP SPEED
500SL: 140mph (225kmh)

0–60mph
500SL: 6.8 sec

LEFT
Between 1971 and 1989 Mercedes-Benz SLs were sold with many different engines, but it was always the large-capacity vee-8 types which made the headlines. The Roadster sold especially well in warm climates, but the lift-off hardtop was an extremely popular option.

By any standards, technical, visual or commercial, the Mercedes-Benz SL models built between 1971 and 1989 were enormously successful. At the start of this period the cars used a newly-designed V8 engine, but as the years passed by the engine was developed, enlarged, considerably lightened, and made more fuel efficient.

Along the way the SL was kept ahead of every safety and emissions reduction law, the result being a car which sold better at the end of its career than it had in the beginning.

Over the years, many different types of this SL family were built, some with 6-cylinder engines, some with V8s, some with manual and some with automatic transmission. In addition, there were two wheelbase lengths, the shorter cars being 2+2-seater open cars, with optional detachable hardtops, longer cars having four seats and a permanent steel roof.

All were big and comparatively beefy cars, with supple all-independent suspension, disc brakes all round, and a full range of equipment. Most important of all, they were built in West Germany with fanatical attention to build quality and detail.

The V8 engine was given a light-alloy cylinder block for the 1980s, and at the same time a 304CID (4973cc) engine size became available. This size was retained throughout the 1980s, but for 1986 there was a further revision, with the V8 engine once again being enlarged, this time to no less than 339CID (5547cc).

Thus the mighty 560SL was born, a car sold only in the USA. If some of the emission laws had not taken their toll of power outputs, this massive unit could have been much more powerful, but in USA-tune it was limited to 230bhp. The frustrating thing for American buyers was that they could see that the European-tune 500SL, though fitted with a smaller engine, actually had more power and more performance.

Even so, it was a very torquey engine indeed, and, when matched to superlative 4-speed automatic transmissions, it provided a remarkable package.

The 560SL, like all cars in this family, had an uncompromisingly square nose, which naturally featured the famous three-pointed star, a deep windscreen, and all possible luxury and functional equipment in the cockpit, and was the sort of car which could swish smoothly and reliably along the autobahns of Europe, or creep without temperament along the crowded city streets of Los Angeles, Chicago and New York City.

Mercedes-Benz knew, of course, that other cars were faster, and that other cars looked better, but it was convinced that no other machine was built so well, or did everything with such aplomb. If power can be equated with capability, then this breed of Mercedes-Benz was always a front-runner.

ABOVE
One of the very last 1970s/1980s SLs ever built, this was a 1989 UK-market 500SL Roadster. The lines had changed very little in an 18-year career.

There was a choice of straight 6-cylinder, or V8 cylinder engines, both being direct developments of existing designs, but both now having twin-overhead-camshaft cylinder heads, with four valves per cylinder.

The latest V8 engine, therefore, though still a 304CID (4973cc) unit, was rated at no less than 326bhp – one third more powerful than the old 2-valve engine which it replaced – and it was backed by a 4-speed automatic transmission. There was no manual transmission alternative.

Because the new SL was so much more powerful than the old, and because it had a much more aerodynamically efficient body shell, it was potentially much faster. German car makers, however, had got together and agreed that such monstrous top speeds were anti-social, so although the car could have achieved more than 170mph (273kmh), its engine was electronically limited, in top gear, to the equivalent of 155mph (250kmh).

All in all, this was an expensive but magnificently detailed machine, giving the impression that Mercedes-Benz's Teutonic thoroughness had forgotten nothing.

BELOW
The 3-pointed star has appeared on the nose of every Mercedes-Benz model built since the merger of 1926.

RIGHT
The new-generation SL of 1989 was not only a very fast two-seater, but it was as docile and reliable as any other Mercedes-Benz family car, with comfortable seating, and a lot of stowage accommodation.

BOTTOM RIGHT
It took five years to develop the new-generation SL, not only to get the shape right, but to make the engines totally 'green' and to make the cars as safe as possible.

Mercedes-Benz SL

PRODUCTION SPAN
Introduced in 1989

ENGINE
6-cyl or V8-cyl, 2 ohc

CAPACITY
181CID (2960cc), 304CID (4973cc)

MAXIMUM POWER
190, 231 or 326bhp

CHASSIS SUSPENSION
Unit construction steel structure, coil spring/wishbone ifs, coil spring/multi-link irs

BODY STYLE
2-door, 2-seater roadster or coupé

TOP SPEED
326bhp: 155mph (250kmh)

0—60mph
326bhp: 6.2 sec

ABOVE
Fanatical attention to detail made the 1989 Mercedes-Benz SL an extremely well-presented supercar for the 1990s. In its initial form it was a two-seater with soft-top or hard-top equipment.

Critics suggest that the modern range of Mercedes-Benz SL models should have been launched years earlier than it was. Maybe so, but the wait was worthwhile. After years of meticulous development, the 1989 variety of SL was recognized as a beautifully developed and outstandingly engineered machine.

The new car, known at Mercedes-Benz as the R129 SL, was developed over a five year period, with a completely new 2-seater structure, new chassis components and substantially re-designed engines.

As one might expect from Mercedes-Benz, the car was immediately recognisable, for the three-pointed star was still an important feature of the front grille. The body style was even smoother than the style which it replaced, the structure was massively strong, and there was a choice of open roadster or (detachable) hardtop derivatives.

The soft top, naturally, was power-operated, the makers boasting that no fewer than 15 hydraulic pumps and 17 microswitches were needed to achieve this in the appropriate manner. The steering wheel was electrically adjustable, for reach and height. There was even a retractable roll-over bar which automatically raised itself if sensors detected sudden deceleration which meant that an accident was beginning to happen.

Both front and rear suspension were developed versions of those used in the smaller Mercedes-Benz saloon models (the 190s, and the medium-sized cars collectively known as W124s). One feature special to the new car, however, was an electronically monitored damping layout which changed settings according to the way the car was being driven. In addition, there was automatic control of suspension ride heights which, for instance, meant that the body was lowered by 0.6in when the car exceeded 75mph (120kmh).

ABOVE
Mercedes-Benz are sometimes said to build the best cars in the world. The new-generation SL model was certainly well-equipped, and carefully assembled.

BELOW
In shaping the 1989 SL, Mercedes-Benz spent hundreds of hours in the wind-tunnel, reducing the drag to a practical minimum. Even so, the identity, and the famous three-pointed star, were faithfully preserved.

Oldsmobile Toronado

PRODUCTION SPAN
1965–1970

ENGINE
V8-cyl, ohv

CAPACITY
425CID (6965cc), or 455CID (7455cc)

MAXIMUM POWER
350–400bhp

CHASSIS SUSPENSION
Separate steel chassis, torsion bar/
wishbone ifs, leaf spring/beam axle rear
suspension

BODY STYLE
2-door, 5-seater coupé

TOP SPEED
385bhp: 425CID model: 126mph
(203kmh)

0–60mph
8.7 sec

The Oldsmobile Toronado was GM's
first-ever front-wheel-drive car, and
was a basic design also modified by
Cadillac for its own use. There was a
big vee-8 engine and automatic
transmission up front, with a long
bonnet, and a compact four-seater
cabin. This was the 1970 version of
the design.

When General Motors launched the front-wheel-drive Oldsmobile Toronado in the autumn of 1965, it was described as the 'most unique American motor car in many years'. It certainly was – it was the first front-wheel-drive car to be built in the USA since the Cord of the 1930s.

Backed by the resources of GM, Oldsmobile had completely re-thought the layout of the front-wheel-drive motor car. Instead of having engine, gearbox and final drive in a neat line, as the Europeans might have done it, Oldsmobile chose to put the engine between the wheels, above the line of the drive shafts, and to have the automatic gearbox alongside, and under the line of, the engine.

The connection between the two was a 2in (5cm) wide silent-running and rubber-damped chain.

Because the new Toronado had to be the flagship of the late-1960s Oldsmobile range, it was given the largest possible engine. This was the bulky but impressive 'big block' engine which Oldsmobile cars had been using since 1957, at first in 425CID/7.0-litre guise, with a downdraught four-barrel carburettor, pushing out no less than 385bhp (SAE). From 1968 the engine became even larger and more powerful, at 455CID and 400bhp.

This was the type of engine which Detroit produced so magnificently and in such large quantities in the 1950s and 1960s. Even when neglected, and serviced only at an owner's whim, such a V8 could rumble on and on for many years, turning out huge amounts of power, but drinking up copious quantities of cheap petrol.

The original Toronado ran on a 119in (302cm) wheelbase chassis frame, this being retained until 1970, when a 4in (10cm) wheelbase stretch and a restyled body made it a larger and less exciting car to drive. Although it was a large and heavy car – in 1966 it was 17ft 7in (5.35m) long, and weighed in at more than 4500lb (2040kg) at the kerbside – it had a well-developed chassis, with torsion bar independent front suspension.

By North American car standards it had a real sporting character, and the smooth styling backed this up. Though large, with an exceedingly long bonnet, it had sleek lines, a 5-seater cabin, and a nicely detailed sloping tail.

By any standards the Toronado was a successful car, nicely and carefully developed, fast, reasonably economical and fun to drive. It was no wonder that 41,000 were sold in the first model year alone, and annual sales soon settled down to around 25,000 cars.

It was a real honour for Oldsmobile that Cadillac picked up the same basic design to use as the Cadillac Eldorado in future years.

TOP
By 1969, the Toronado had made its mark, was selling well, and had been lightly facelifted.

ABOVE LEFT
The original Toronado, launched as a 1966 model, had smart rounded lines.

LEFT
Except that the Toronado had a slightly longer nose than many other Detroit models, no-one could know that it had front-wheel-drive.

RIGHT
GM's particular solution to the front-wheel-drive layout was to put the massive Oldsmobile vee-8 between the front wheels, with the transmission under, and to one side, of it. It was a brave technological move, which worked well.

Pegaso Z102

PRODUCTION SPAN
1951–1958

ENGINE
V8-cyl, 2 ohc

CAPACITY
151CID (2474cc), 172CID (2816cc), and 194CID (3178cc)

MAXIMUM POWER
140–275bhp

CHASSIS SUSPENSION
Steel platform-type chassis, torsion bar/wishbone ifs, torsion bar/De Dion rear suspension

BODY STYLE
2-door, 2-seater coupé or convertible, various

TOP SPEED
165bhp 2.5-litre: 120mph (193kmh)

0–60mph
11.0 sec

Wilfred Ricart's Pegaso was the first and, so far, the only supercar to be built in post-war Spain. Introduced in 1951, it was never meant to be a quantity-production car, but was really a hand-built prestige project at ENASA, a nationalised Spanish concern which mainly built trucks, buses and public service vehicles. Only 110 Z102s were ever built, and very few survive to this day.

Ricard himself was a Spanish engineer who had designed the Nacional Pescara in the 1920s, had been the head of Alfa-Romeo's research department in the late 1930s, and was technical director during the Second World War.

The Pegaso car project was designed to draw attention to everything that the Spanish concern could do, and was built under tool-room conditions. Accordingly, although the same basic V8 engine was always used, over the years it was produced in three different sizes at power ratings varying between 140bhp/2.5-litres, and 275bhp/3.2-litres with supercharging.

In each case the engine had twin overhead camshaft cylinder heads, in a layout which drew heavily on Ricart's own experience at Alfa Romeo, matched to a 5-speed

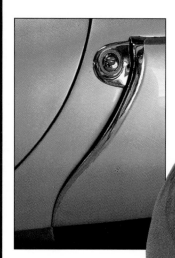

A B O V E
The stylist's attention to detail on Spain's most exclusive car.

non-synchromesh gearbox. This combination powered a complex steel platform-style chassis frame featuring De Dion rear suspension. The chassis was specifically designed to be fabricated, not built from pressed members, in the ENASA tool rooms.

Because the cars were all hand-built, a variety of 2-seater bodies were fitted, some with factory-approved styles by Saoutchik and Touring coachwork. Each of these cars was blessed with a 3-year warranty.

The Pegaso's rev counter, reading up to 8,500rpm, also found space for the ammeter.

ABOVE
Every Pegaso Z102 was hand-built, to tool-room standards of accuracy, then graced with a carefully coachbuilt body style. Vee-8 engines of up to 275bhp were fitted.

As with the Ferraris of the day, the Pegaso was not a car one bought to use as everyday transport (however fast), but as a show-off machine, preferably for leisure purposes. The only mistake Ricart made, in the opinion of some pundits, was to choose an 8-cylinder engine, when his major competitor (Ferrari) used V12s.

The lucky (and wealthy) few who purchased a Pegaso Z102 did not seem to mind this, for although they now had a car which lacked development in some details, the most powerful derivatives were among the fastest cars in the world in the early 1950s, when the major competition came from Ferrari and Mercedes-Benz.

Wilfred Ricart left ENASA in 1959, after which the Pegaso passenger car business was rapidly closed down.

BELOW
The Pegaso's vee-8 engine had a unique layout of staggered twin-choke carburettors.

RIGHT
You don't see many of those badges!
The Pegaso was, and remains, one of
the world's rarest cars.

ABOVE
Not only was the Pegaso very
carefully engineered, but the cars
had beautiful styling. There were
many different styles – with this
coupé having something in common
with Ferraris of the period.

LEFT
The Pegaso's interior, like that of
Ferraris of the period, was simple,
but well-equipped. The major
instruments – speedometer and rev-
counter, were large, and well-
presented ahead of the driver's eyes.

Porsche 911 Turbo

PRODUCTION SPAN
1975–1989

ENGINE
Flat 6-cyl, ohc

CAPACITY
181CID (2993cc), or 304CID (3299cc)

MAXIMUM POWER
260 or 300bhp

CHASSIS SUSPENSION
Unit construction steel structure, torsion bar/wishbone ifs, torsion bar/semi-trailing arm irs

BODY STYLE
2-door, 4-seater coupé, Targa coupé, or convertible,

TOP SPEED
3.3-litre: 156mph (251kmh)

0–60mph
3.3-litre: 4.9 sec

Even though the 911 Turbo of the 1980s used a body style which was more than 20 years old, it was still an extremely purposeful and finely-detailed car with a top speed of more than 150mph.

By the mid-1980s, Porsche enthusiasts were beginning to think that the famous 911 Turbo would be around forever, but in the end it was dropped in 1989, after a phenomenally successful run.

The original Porsches were based on the VW Beetle underpan and running gear, which is to say that they had air-cooled 'flat' engines mounted in the tail, driving the rear wheels. Although the 911 series, first seen in 1963, retained this concept, it was larger, smoother, more powerful, faster and entirely different in detail. In this case the engine was a flat six, but it was still air-cooled, still in the tail, and still driving the rear wheels.

The first 911s had normally-aspirated 2.0-litre/122CID engines, but in the next decade these grew to 3.0-litres/181CID, and became more powerful. Along the way, Porsche also developed the chassis, refined the aerodynamics, and provided different body styles.

In the early 1970s Porsche developed turbocharged versions of the flat-six engine to use in motor racing, and for 1975 a civilised version was installed in the road car. This was the first of the legendary 911 Turbo models, a car which had 3.0-litres/181CID, 260bhp and quite phenomenal performance. It had so much torque that the existing gearbox could not stand the strain, so a new 4-speed transmission was designed.

By the mid-1980s the long-running 911 Turbo was available in closed and open form, as this Cabriolet makes clear. The number plate – owned by the British Porsche concessionaires – tells its own story.

BELOW
Most 911 Turbos are driven so fast that other drivers cannot pick out the 'Turbo' on the engine compartment panel, below the rear spoiler.

Less than three years later the engine was enlarged to 3.3-litres/304CID, produced 300bhp, and Porsche offered true supercar performance which was barely matched by much larger and more expensive rivals.

The engine installation was remarkable in many ways, for the engine bay was in the tail, well away from ram cooling air, and surrounded by close-fitting panelling. Air-cooling was achieved by a large fan built onto the engine itself, while the engine oil was circulated through another cooler to add to heat transfer. Porsche, being diligent West Germans, seemed to have thought of everything, the result being that the Turbo built an impressive reliability record.

The car had enormous character – a combination of style, flat-out performance, Teutonic efficiency and that unforgettable gruff engine note. But the roadholding was by no means top class. Taken through corners in the wrong way,

LEFT
This was the original 260bhp, 3-litre 911 Turbo, complete with wider wheels and tyres, and the large tail spoiler. The difference in character, and the more purposeful stance, is immediately obvious.

and at the wrong speeds, a Turbo could bite back, spinning viciously, and hard. Not many drivers could recover once the process had started.

So far as possible, Porsche trimmed the chassis and aerodynamic balance to suit the power, though it was asking a lot for a car with such a rearward weight bias to behave perfectly in all conditions. Compared with other Porsches, however, the Turbo had wider wheels and tyres, particularly at the rear, where large wheelarch extensions were needed to cover them up, and there was a large spoiler to provide nett downforce at high speeds.

Such performance, of course, could rarely be used on most public roads, but in West Germany, where there was no autobahn speed limit, 911 Turbos could regularly be seen scudding along at 130mph (209kmh) and more. An outstanding car would be needed to replace the 911 Turbo, and for the 1990s Porsche was rumoured to be preparing a new generation four-wheel-drive car.

BELOW
Body modifications added in the UK by Porsche specialists Autofarm make this Turbo look even fiercer than usual. For normal day-time motoring the headlamps would be hidden under the droop nose.

Porsche 959

PRODUCTION SPAN
1986–1988

ENGINE
Flat 6-cyl, 2 ohc

CAPACITY
174CID (2850cc)

MAXIMUM POWER
450bhp

CHASSIS SUSPENSION
Unit construction steel structure, torsion bar/wishbone ifs, torsion bar/wishbone irs

BODY STYLE
2-door, 2-seater coupé

TOP SPEED
196mph (315kmh)

0–60mph
3.9 sec

You only have to quote a type number – 959 – for motoring enthusiasts to identify a Porsche. In 1987, when it went on sale, the 959 was the fastest, most complex and most expensive Porsche yet sold.

It started life as a competition car, for use in Group B motorsport, where the regulations asked for only 200 cars to be produced. Between 1983, when the first prototype was shown, and 1986, when development was nearly complete, the rules of motorsport changed (Group B cars were banned from rallying), so Porsche concentrated on making the 959 a superlative road machine.

The roots of the 959 lay in the conventional rear-engined 911, but although the production 959 used a much-modified 911 structure and rear-mounted flat-six engine, it was different in almost every other way. Superficially, the 959 looked like a 911 with different aerodynamic features, including a 'ring' type of spoiler on the tail along with vastly enlarged wheelarches to cover the wide tyres, though much of the shell featured lightweight, advanced composite materials instead of conventional pressed-steel panels. It was, of course, no longer than a conventional 911 or 911 Turbo although it had much wider wheel tracks.

The vital chassis difference was the use of permanent four-wheel-drive, while the 959 also used a twin-turbo-charged engine (one turbo actually blowing through the other) with water-cooled cylinder heads and four valves per cylinder. The engine had originally been used in the Type 956 and 962 race cars, where 650–700bhp was possible, so with mild-boost, and 450bhp, it was ultra-reliable for the 959 road car application.

The 959's truly advanced feature, however, was its sophisticated four-wheel-drive layout, which had variable front/torque split, was matched to a 6-speed synchromesh gear-

TOP RIGHT
The 959 was Porsche's most complex car, not only because of its four-wheel-drive, but because of the six-speed gearbox, and all the electronic controls which monitored the transmission too.

BELOW
The Porsche 959 looked good from every angle. Some parts of the 911 body shell were used, but the 959 had a smoother nose, a longer tail, sills under the doors, and special wheels, all to make it distinctive.

L E F T
The 959 was a very well-balanced supercar, with exceptional grip and remarkable handling.

box, and had electronic control and monitoring of limited-slip differentials. Fat tyres, ABS anti-lock braking, and power-assisted steering all helped give the 959 a superlative chassis. By any reckoning, the 959 was probably the best all-round car in the world in the late 1980s.

It was the very first 911-family Porsche with no handling vices, and it had superb traction and cornering grip. This was allied to sensational performance where the top speed approached 200mph (322kmh), and amazing docility, which allowed it to be driven slowly and haltingly in heavy traffic.

Group B cars, in general, were difficult to sell (even the road car versions were often too uncivilised and too temperamental for general use), but the 200 production 959s were sold out well before production began. By the end of 1988, when the last car was delivered, secondhand 959s were changing hands for as much as three times their original values.

ACKNOWLEDGEMENTS

The author and publishers would like to thank the automobile companies who have kindly provided images and information for this book. All illustrations are from those companies' own archives, from the J Baker Collection, and from the National Motor Museum, Beaulieu.